"Kelli Sandman-Hurley has been and is my 'go to person' when I have a question on dyslexia. Her knowledge of dyslexia is truly extensive and her championing for children is well-known in California and other states as well. Kelli takes every opportunity to work on behalf of children with dyslexia, from working directly with parents and children to schools and speaking at legislative hearings. I continue to seek her advice and often refer parents from across the country to reach out to Kelli for assistance when they are in need of expert advice on issues of dyslexia."

—Vaughn K. Lauer PhD, Educational Learning and Training, LLC, author of When the School Says No…How to Get the Yes!

"Dr. Sandman-Hurley is spot on when she says 'advocating for a student with dyslexia requires you to raise awareness about dyslexia.' This book is a great resource to help parents and professionals do both!"

—Deborah Lynam, Parent, Decoding Dyslexia NJ

of related interest

A Guide to Special Education Advocacy
What Parents, Clinicians and Advocates Need to Know
Matthew Cohen
ISBN 978 1 84310 893 1
eISBN 978 1 84642 921 7

When the School Says No…How to Get the Yes!
Securing Special Education Services for Your Child
Vaughn K. Lauer
ISBN 978 1 84905 917 6
eISBN 978 0 85700 664 6

Can I tell you about Dyslexia?
A guide for friends, family and professionals
Alan M. Hultquist
Illustrated by Bill Tulp
ISBN 978 1 84905 952 7
eISBN 978 0 85700 810 7

DYSLEXIA ADVOCATE!

HOW TO ADVOCATE FOR A CHILD WITH DYSLEXIA WITHIN THE PUBLIC EDUCATION SYSTEM

Kelli Sandman-Hurley

Jessica Kingsley *Publishers*
London and Philadelphia

First published in 2016
by Jessica Kingsley Publishers
73 Collier Street
London N1 9BE, UK
and
400 Market Street, Suite 400
Philadelphia, PA 19106, USA

www.jkp.com

Library of Congress Cataloging in Publication Data
Names: Sandman-Hurley, Kelli.
Title: Dyslexia advocate! : how to advocate for a child with dyslexia within
    the public education system / Kelli Sandman-Hurley.
Description: Philadelphia, PA : Jessica Kingsley Publishers, 2016. | Includes
    bibliographical references and index.
Identifiers: LCCN 2015040989 | ISBN 9781849057370
Subjects: LCSH: Dyslexia. | Individualized education program--United States.
    | Children with disabilities--Education--Law and legislation--United
    States.
Classification: LCC LB1050.5 .S225 2016 | DDC 371.91/44--dc23 LC record available at
http://lccn.loc.gov/2015040989

British Library Cataloguing in Publication Data
A CIP catalogue record for this book is available from the British Library

ISBN 978 1 84905 737 0
eISBN 978 1 78450 274 4

Printed and bound in the Unites States

Certified Chain of Custody
SUSTAINABLE   Promoting Sustainable Forestry
FORESTRY
INITIATIVE   www.sfiprogram.org
SFI-01268

SFI label applies to the text stock

To Rick and Casey. You so generously let me take time from our family so that I could follow my passion and help other families. Thank you and I love you.

To the adults I worked with at READ/San Diego of the San Diego Public Library. You are the reason I do what I do. I am sorry I met you after you became adults and I was not able to help you before your struggles with literacy brought you to READ/San Diego. But your stories moved me to do something more. Thank you for sharing your stories with me. Never give up.

Finally, to the parents of the students who have sat in my office and cried, screamed, complained and felt so alone, you are my inspiration. You refuse to give up on your bright children and you called for change. Change is coming and it is all because you refused to let your children be the victims of what could be the civil rights issue of our time.

To the great people who took the time to read this book and offer feedback, specifically Tracy, Brittany, Vaughn, and Jenifer, I appreciate you!

To my dad, who has forever been my editor with the most honest feedback. To my mom, for always being proud of me.

Dyslexia is real.

CONTENTS

PREFACE

ad + voce + ate → Advocate—Add your voice

/T/ /t/ /taw/ /tawn/ /tawm/ Tom sag the sssooonnng, song, song to kid.

Nathan is trying to read the following sentence: *Tom sang the song to the kids.* Listening to Nathan read is painful. He struggles through one- and two-syllable words, he skips words like a, and, the, of, if, and often ignores punctuation. He reads with no expression and often can't remember what he just read, but sometimes surprisingly understands everything he read. He is inconsistent with his reading. His spelling is almost incomprehensible. He often spells <pad> either <bad> or <pat>. He will spell longer words like <every> as <evry>, <plane> as <playn> or <billed> as <billd>. However, when you read something to him or he listens to something in an audio format, he can tell you every detail and usually add his own commentary. He is very bright. He has a great verbal vocabulary and is creative—and he is about to go into the fourth grade reading at a first grade level. So, why can't he read? In one word, dyslexia. But Nathan is just one example of how dyslexia might affect a student. Some students with dyslexia might be decent readers and poor spellers. Others might only need more time to read to understand what they read. And still others might not be able to read or spell even the simplest words. They are all different children, with different symptoms, but they all have dyslexia.

Dyslexia is real. In every school, in every city in this country and beyond, are students (approximately one in five) who go to school every day and wonder why their friends seem to learn to read and spell without a problem. They ask themselves why they can't, and in many cases, they begin to question their own intelligence. They are labeled lazy, unmotivated, slow, or late bloomers. They struggle when asked to read in front of their peers and require at least twice as much time for homework than their fellow students. They may study for hours in preparation for spelling tests, only to misspell the same words two weeks later. They repeatedly get their papers returned with red marks, even after hours of studying, yet they understand information that is presented to them in auditory format. They have great story recall and can retell and add critical commentary to anything that is read to them. They try and they try, but they need someone to teach them differently. That is all they need—someone to present the information in a different way than the traditional "open your brain and let the teachers pour the information in," which simply will not work for students with dyslexia. They need an intervention that responds to their individual needs.

According to the International Dyslexia Association (IDA) and Shelly Shaywitz (2003), dyslexia affects up to 20 percent of the population. It affects boys and girls alike. It does not discriminate on the basis of race, religion, economic or social status. It does not come and go. It's not a symptom of laziness or a lack of motivation. It cannot be cured, because it is not a disease. However, those with dyslexia can overcome it with the right educational plan, the right intervention, highly trained teachers, and a lot of support from family, friends, teachers, administrators, and advocates, who all must embrace the reality of dyslexia and the intellectual capability of a student with dyslexia.

If you have found your way to this book, you have probably done a lot of research looking for reliable information about dyslexia or maybe you even read the book, *Overcoming Dyslexia*, by Sally Shaywitz. You may be at a point where you are asking yourself, "Okay, I know what dyslexia is, I know that my child, my student, or my relative probably has dyslexia and I understand that my child needs an intervention that is based on a structured literacy approach, so how do I work with the school to provide the Free Appropriate Public Education (FAPE) my student is entitled to?" That's when this book comes in handy.

This book is intended to help you navigate your way through the public school system when you are advocating for a student with dyslexia. This may be your own child, your grandchild, niece or nephew. This book is also a good fit for special education advocates and attorneys who are advocating for students with dyslexia. Finally, this book is for teachers and administrators in the hope that they will learn how to help these students and make their academic careers easier for them and their families.

This book is also meant to be a resource that you can refer to time and again. The table of contents should guide you to the pages that will help you through your current stage in the process. One key principle I would like to leave you with is this: Advocating for a student with dyslexia requires you to raise awareness about dyslexia. You will be spending a significant amount of your time educating those involved in your student's education about dyslexia and interventions for dyslexia, as well as writing goals for students with dyslexia, tracking progress, and providing resources to help those involved understand dyslexia. It will be your journey to create change through awareness. Your job will be to provide the dyslexia awareness that is not provided in teacher education, Master's degree education or continuing education (professional development) but that is needed to give an appropriate education for students with dyslexia.

Every student with dyslexia has individual needs and it would be impossible for this book to address every possible scenario. The purpose of the book is to provide you with basic information to help you through the process of determining if your child is eligible for special education services, finding appropriate services, and keeping up with the services, but you will also need to take the time to research your state's regulations, and establish your student's individual needs. Be aware that all states have to follow 2004 Individuals with Disabilities Education Act (IDEA) statute and regulations and when a state adds any additional regulations, those state regulations may not take away a right provided by the federal statute and regulations. State regulations may provide additional details and specific procedures that can supplement the federal statute and regulations. (To find your state's regulations, you can do an internet search of your state's name + special education regulations.) As you read this book you may notice the following words used a lot: usually, can, may, possibly, might, etc. These words were chosen very carefully, because advocacy is not a one-size-fits-all process. This book is also not legal advice; it is written from the viewpoint of a non-attorney advocate who advocates for students with dyslexia. At some point in your journey you may need legal advice, and that is when you should contact a special education attorney.

In the Appendix you will find a list of the IDEA regulations and their complete entries that are mentioned throughout the book. Before each regulation is a brief description of what the regulation explains. It might be helpful to use the Appendix to help you through the process.

Expect bumps in the road, tears, and frustration along the way, but the trip to an effective and appropriate education for your child is worth the trials and tribulations. Remember, each child has unique, individual needs, and though parents/guardians of children with dyslexia share many of the same experiences during this process, there will be nuances in each case. There is not one way to advocate. You have to negotiate and navigate according to your current situation. There is no one "right" path to take, but with a solid understanding of the IDEA you will know which path is yours.

CHAPTER 1

What is Dyslexia?

Try reading the following:

> The bottob line it thit it doet exitt, no bitter whit nibe teotle give it (i.e. ttecific leirning ditibility, etc.). In fict, iccording to Tilly Thiywitz (2003) itt trevilence it ictuilly one in five children, which it twenty tercent.

How was it? Did you stumble on some words? Did you skip words and or substitute with "whatever" or "something?" Based on experience, I am going to guess that this was not easy for you. I will guess that if I asked you to read this in front of your peers, who are prone to judgement, you would feel anxious. I am also going to guess that if I asked you to tell me what you learned from the passage, you wouldn't be able to recall any important information. Now imagine that you are required to read the rest of this book and it is written just like the opening sentences. Would you do it? Or would it seem impossible?

You just experienced what it feels like to have dyslexia for one minute. During that minute, the passage slowed you down and forced you to pronounce words that didn't seem to make any sense and weren't familiar to you. You knew they were wrong, but you read them anyway. And how about that time factor? Did you feel pressed for time? If you were in a classroom full of your peers and I asked you to read this aloud and then asked comprehension questions, would your heart rate go up? Would you suddenly have to use the restroom? Or perhaps you would need to go to the nurse with a stomach ache? This is dyslexia.

The word dyslexia has been used, abused, and misused throughout the years, which has made teachers, administrators, and school psychologists resistant to using it, but dyslexia does have specific characteristics associated with it. The bottom line is that it does exist, no matter what name people give it (i.e. specific learning disability, etc.). In fact, according to the International Dyslexic Association (IDA) and Sally Shaywitz (2003) its prevalence is actually one in five children, which is 20 percent. Think about that. Twenty percent of the school population has dyslexia—to some degree. Now think about this, autism affects 1 in 68 children and we hear about autism all the time. Dyslexia is a neurobiological difference in the brain that makes reading and writing more difficult to learn. Remember that reading and writing are manmade constructs and not every brain has the ability to learn those constructs as readily as others, without explicit instruction. What this means for teachers is that every single year in every single class of 20 students or more sit at least four students with a high probability of having dyslexia. Dyslexia can manifest differently in each student. Some may have extreme difficulty with decoding. Some may read accurately, yet slowly, and then cannot tell you what they read. Others may read well enough to keep up, but be poor spellers. Some may read a little slowly. Most students with dyslexia have a difficult time composing written compositions. These are all symptoms of dyslexia. Dyslexia also occurs on a continuum; it may be mild in one student and severe in another. But this is the annotated description of dyslexia. The IDA provides the following definition:

Dyslexia is characterized by difficulties with accurate and/ or fluent word recognition and by poor spelling and decoding abilities. These difficulties typically result from a deficit in the phonological component of language that is often unexpected in relation to other cognitive abilities and the provision of effective classroom instruction. Secondary consequences may include problems in reading comprehension and reduced reading experience that can impede growth of vocabulary and background knowledge. (Adopted by the IDA Board of Directors, November 12, 2002; this definition is also used by the National Institute of Child Health and Human Development)

Dyslexia, in the simplest terms, is a difficulty with phonological and orthographic processing which can make it challenging to decode (read) and encode (spell) words, comprehend what has been read, and write sentences and longer compositions. There is also double-deficit dyslexia, where people struggle with rapid naming, which means they find it difficult to name things (letters, numbers, objects, etc.) quickly and efficiently, which makes fluency more difficult to improve.

Dyslexia and the brain

In very simplistic terms, researchers using sophisticated imaging technology (such as functional magnetic resonance imaging, fMRI) have been able to identify areas of the brain that are most active during a reading activity. Researchers have then used this neural signature for reading and compared that signature to the brains of students with dyslexia, identifying that students with dyslexia do not use the reading areas of the brain as efficiently as those without dyslexia. Interestingly, researchers have also discovered that students with dyslexia utilize the right hemisphere of their brain during reading activities more than those who do not have dyslexia. Additionally, there is evidence that with appropriate intervention the brains of those with dyslexia begin to function more like those without dyslexia during reading tasks.

Signs and symptoms of dyslexia

The following is a list of signs and symptoms of dyslexia. While you are reading through this list it is important to understand that there is not one profile for a student with dyslexia. Dyslexia occurs on a continuum and can be mild to moderate to severe to profound. One child with dyslexia might have extreme difficulty with basic reading tasks, while another may be able to decode but has difficulty with spelling, and another might have trouble with reading fluency. It is extremely important to determine the strengths and weaknesses of each individual in order to work out what is appropriate for them to improve their literacy skills.

- *Difficulty decoding words in isolation*: This is difficulty reading words out of context, usually in lists. This is often more difficult for children with dyslexia because they have to rely on their knowledge of the structure of English to decode isolated words instead of guessing the word based on context when it presented within a sentence or passage.

- *Difficulty spelling (orthography)*: Children with dyslexia almost always struggle with spelling and are usually relying on the one-to-one sound-to-symbol relationship to spell words rather than an understanding of English orthography. For example, they might spell <spilled> as <spild> or <spilld>.

- *Difficulty with phonemic awareness*: Phonemic awareness is the ability of the student to verbally manipulate language before graphemes are presented. For example, the student may have difficulty understanding, or articulating, that the word <cat> has three phonemes, /c/ /a/ /t/ and may instead say it the following way /c/ /at/.

- *Difficulty with phonological awareness*: Phonological awareness is the ability to manipulate language when graphemes are presented. For example, give the student the word <cat> and ask them to tell you to remove the <c> and then pronounce the letter string that remains, which would be <at>.

- *Slow, laborious reading*: Children with dyslexia might read a passage or sentence very slowly, trying to decode (sound out) each and every word. This is especially prominent when larger, polysyllabic words are included in the text.

- *Difficulty with math word problems*: A child with dyslexia who is struggling with reading will also struggle to read math problems.

- *Reversing letters beyond second grade*: The reversal of b and d, as well as other letters, is normal through first grade, but after that it becomes an indicator that the child might be at risk for dyslexia.

A child with dyslexia needs a structured, multisensory, explicit intervention

The one thing a child with dyslexia absolutely does not need is the "eclectic" approach to teaching reading, which is a little bit of this and a little bit of that. English is a rules-based language that makes sense when the underlying structure is taught and studied. When a child with dyslexia is taught the structure of the language with a structured, multisensory, explicit, and systematic approach, they improve their reading and spelling. There are two approaches to consider: the Orton-Gillingham approach and Structured Word Inquiry.

But, what is a structured, multisensory, explicit approach? Well, read on to find out…

Let's take care of a few basics first:

- An intervention for students with dyslexia should include etymology, morphology, and phonology in a structured, multisensory, and explicit way.

- Orton-Gillingham is an approach, not a methodology. There are many programs that were developed based on the Orton-Gillingham approach, such as the *Wilson Reading System* and the *Barton Reading and Spelling* program (see the IDA Matrix for additional programs—more information is provided in the References section at the end of the book, under "Websites"). The Orton-Gillingham approach itself is not owned by any company or organization.

- Anyone working with a student using the Orton-Gillingham approach should be trained, and this training requires a supervised, practical element. Three hours or one day of training is not sufficient.

- Structured Word Inquiry (SWI) is also an approach to teaching the underlying structure of English and is based on the student's inquiry and investigation into the morphophonemic nature of English via the study of etymology, meaning, and the phonology of words.

- Spelling and the grammatical categories of words to help understand spelling should be a integral and central part of any intervention.

STRUCTURED INTERVENTION

Students with dyslexia require a structured intervention. The Oxford Dictionary defines structured as, "The arrangement of and relations between the parts or elements of something complex." And if English isn't complex then I don't know what is. For a student with dyslexia, this means that the person implementing the program understands what a student needs to know about one part of English before they can successfully move on to the next. For example, a first grade student may need to know that the grapheme <c> can represent more than one phoneme, /k/ and /s/, like the word <circus>, before they move on to the different phonemes of <g> which are /g/ and /j/. They will also learn that digraphs like <ch> can represent three different phonemes before they can decode a word like <chef>. In the Orton-Gillingham approach, the structured requirement is fulfilled by teaching syllable types (six or seven syllable types depending on which program is being used) in order. When using SWI, this requirement is fulfilled by having students become proficient at finding bases, recurring spelling patterns, and affixes, and applying that knowledge to increasingly difficult words.

MULTISENSORY INTERVENTION

Students with dyslexia require an intervention that is also multisensory. The multisensory part of the instruction is often missing from curricula developed by big publishers of reading programs for struggling students. The Oxford Dictionary defines multisensory as, "Involving or using more than one of the senses." The senses in this case include hearing, seeing, and tactile/kinesthetic. This idea runs contrary to the fill-in-the-worksheet and repeat-after-me scope and sequence of most curricula. If students are receiving a program that is multisensory, they are using more than their eyes and ears to learn. For example, they might be manipulating parts of the language, like bases and affixes, using cards. Or they might be creating flow charts to determine when to drop the single silent <e>. For students with dyslexia who are learning the structure of English, this means they are also manipulating word parts on cards, grapheme (letter) cards, using word matrices and building word sums. For example, a student who is explicitly investigating the word <sign> using multisensory techniques will write out the following word sum, while simultaneously announcing each letter, verbally checking for changes to the base word along the way and then rewriting the word:

sign + al → signal. Then she notices the reason for the <g> in that word. The student will also be manipulating grapheme cards to blend simple words and learn how the phonology of each grapheme blends together to create a pronounceable (readable) word. For example, she will have the grapheme cards <c> <a> <t> out on the table, and using her finger to trace below the word from left to right, she will be able to decode the new word.

EXPLICIT INTERVENTION

Students with dyslexia require an intervention that explicitly teaches the underlying structure of English. Now the word "explicitly" is very important. The Oxford Dictionary defines explicit as, "Stated clearly and in detail, leaving no room for confusion or doubt." This is exactly what an appropriate intervention does for a student with dyslexia; the teacher explains to her exactly why words are spelled and pronounced the way they are, and it leaves no room for confusion. In fact, the student who receives the appropriate, explicit intervention knows why words are spelled the way they are and can explain those reasons to anyone who asks. For example, a properly trained person will be able to explain explicitly to a student why the word <circus> has two different phonemes, /k/ and /s/, represented by one grapheme <c>. They will also be able to explain that the suffix for the word <action> is <-ion> and the base is <act>. They will then take that a step further and notice the phonology change for the grapheme <t> in the word <action> from the related word <acting>. This explicitness leaves the student with less confusion about the structure of the language and having this information helps her understand how to pronounce (read) and spell words with a deep understanding of English orthography.

But the approach is only half the recipe; the teacher needs to be highly trained in order to be effective in helping the student with dyslexia understand English orthography and be able to transfer that understanding into improved reading and spelling. In the dyslexia community, highly trained does not mean one day of training, or even a week-long course.

Unfortunately, neither IDEA nor Every Child Succeeds Act (ESSA) provide a definition for "highly trained." The former term in NCLB, "highly qualified," has been stricken and replaced with "teachers who meet the applicable State certification and licensure requirements" (ESSA Section 9414(c)(2)). Highly trained does not mean that the instructor will be trained in dyslexia or the appropriate intervention. In the dyslexia community, highly trained in structured literacy (e.g. Orton-Gillingham) means the instructor has received training and the training included a supervised, practical element. If the chosen approach is SWI, then the instructor will have deep knowledge of English orthography and how to teach students to understand English with etymology, morphology, and phonology as their guide.

Using computer programs

It is becoming increasingly popular for a student to be offered a computer-based program as an intervention. While supplementing an intervention with some independent practice on a computer, using it in place of an intervention that provides explicitness and an opportunity to talk about the concepts, and ask questions with a highly qualified teacher, is not appropriate. A computer program may be able to adjust to a student's level and understanding, but it cannot provide the direct instruction that a student with dyslexia needs. For example, if a student answers a question on the computer wrong, or wants to know why a word is spelled the way it is, who are they going to ask?

Debunking dyslexia myths

"Students with dyslexia see the letters or words backwards."

Although this has been a running joke on countless sitcoms, comedy stages, and around the dinner table, it is totally untrue. People with dyslexia see letters and words the same way those without dyslexia do; dyslexia is not a vision problem. It cannot be "cured" with covered overlays or vision therapy. In fact, the American Academy of Ophthalmologists states that most tracking problems are a result of dyslexia, not the cause.

Why do we confuse b, d, p, and q anyway? Most of us know that this is a normal part of learning to read. Anyone who has watched a preschooler learn to read has seen her wonder out loud if that is a b or d they are trying to read. We have also seen this same preschooler become a first grader and after a while they just "get it." And then there are those who continue to mix up these letters past second grade. The interesting, and often not answered very well, question is: why? Stanislaus Dehaene, author of *Reading in the Brain* (2010), does a great job of explaining this in a chapter in the book *Dyslexia Across Languages* (2011). I am going to do my best to paraphrase because I think it is important to understand how the brain has adapted to fit reading into a space that was originally meant for other skills.

So, we now know that the brain has adapted to allow us to read. We know from Maryanne Wolf (2008) and Stanislaus Dehaene that the written language was not created arbitrarily but in such a way that our brains could understand. Most letters consist of less than three lines. They were not made with more than that, because our brains could not process those configurations due to the fact that the reading part of our brains was originally wired to do things like recognize faces. Our brains were not built for reading; we had to fit reading into our brains (Wolf 2008).

Back to the mixing up of b, d, p, and q. It just so happens that our brain is naturally wired to be able to determine that a cow is a cow no matter how we see it. If we see it facing left, it's a cow. If we see it facing right, it's still a cow. So when we introduce letters like b and d to the preschooler, she has to unlearn this mirror image ability that is built into the brain.

People with dyslexia see words and letters the same way people without dyslexia do. Therefore any "intervention" that targets the visual (sight) system is misguided. This includes colored paper, covered overlays, colored lenses, and vision therapy. The American Academy of Ophthalmologists released a report about the misuse of vision interventions for students with dyslexia, which explains that it is not productive for the student with dyslexia to try to correct what they see instead of how they process the information. It is a good idea to print off this report and take it with you to meetings so you can show the information to the team when and if they want to offer vision therapy as an intervention for dyslexia (see the References section, "Websites").

"If they read more over the summer, they would improve."

I have seen comments made on the report cards of struggling readers by well-meaning teachers that say something to the effect of, "If she just read more this summer she would improve her reading." or "You just haven't found the right book yet." or "You need to read to her more." To borrow a line from Rick Lavoie from FAT City, the "kid with dyslexia is working harder than anyone else in that class." The student with dyslexia can take twice as long to read as the child without dyslexia. Students with dyslexia do not have an intellectual deficit and, in most cases, they do not have motivational problem (although after years of failure this could come into play); they understand what they read, they have opinions about what they read, they just may not be able to read as quickly. What they need is an intensive intervention implemented by a trained professional, not to be told to read more or to try harder or to work on their motivation. If we offer a student with dyslexia an incentive to read or spell, but the appropriate remediation is not provided, the student is set up for failure. Be careful with incentives. I have yet to meet a student with dyslexia who is not motivated to learn to read and spell.

"Let's wait until third grade to have the child tested."

No, no, no! Dyslexia is not something that is outgrown. In fact, once students hit third grade, or even worse, fourth grade, they are having such difficulty that it may be starting to affect their emotional health. The key to helping someone with dyslexia is to have them identified as early as possible. The introduction of Response to Intervention (RtI) (more about RtI in Chapter 4) is a positive step in the right direction, provided the student is not released from the program too soon, and the chosen intervention is appropriate and implemented with fidelity by an adequately trained professional. But the main point here is that waiting is never a good idea for a child with dyslexia. After all, she should be learning to read when her peers are learning to read, in kindergarten through third grade—after that she is reading to learn. In fact, special education data in California shows that very few students are identified for services under the specific learning disabilities (SLD) category in kindergarten to second grade. There is a significant increase in third and fourth grades, and what is most troubling is that those numbers never decrease. Because most students with SLD are identified late and not provided with the appropriate remediation, they never graduate out of special education. This should not be happening with the information we have today about how to effectively help a student who is struggling with reading and writing. Lyon *et al.* (2001) reported that 80 percent of students identified as having SLD were struggling with reading and spelling. Since dyslexia occurs in up to 20 percent of the population, it isn't too far-fetched to assume that a large percentage of those identified are dyslexic. If this is true, then they should be identified in kindergarten or first grade, receive the appropriate intervention, and graduate out of special education by fourth grade. So, waiting to test does nothing but prolong the issue and cause more academic and emotional harm to the student and unnecessary financial stress on the school.

"Accommodations give an unfair advantage."

Think about this. If a child cannot see well and we give her glasses, does she have an unfair advantage? If a student is in a wheelchair, is allowing her to use the elevator an unfair advantage? If we give a child who isn't reading at grade level due to a reading disability the ability to listen to texts on audio so she now has access to what she is intellectually capable of understanding, is that unfair to the others? If a child writes, "The cat is big" instead of what she would like to write, such as, "The lion with the brilliant golden mane is enormous and ferocious," because she is hindered by spelling, and we provide speech-to-text software so she can write her true thoughts, is that unfair or does that unleash her true potential? It's not an "unfair advantage;" it is leveling the playing field and giving children with dyslexia equal access to grade level content and the ability to produce grade level work.

"Dyslexia is caused by poor teaching or lack of educational opportunity."

Let's meet Joseph for just a minute. Joseph grew up in a wealthy home with his mom and dad. His mom is a pediatrician and his dad has a PhD in Neuroscience from an Ivy League college. Joseph was exposed to reading and a print-rich environment on a daily basis. Joseph never missed school, never had a major illness, and attended a highly rated school in an urban city. But Joseph has dyslexia. No doubt about it. Now consider Jennifer; she is Joseph's sister and has been exposed to the same environment as Joseph, but she does not have dyslexia. The environmental theory does not hold up. Bring in the fMRI studies, which illustrate functional differences in how the brain responds to reading prompts, and you will see the difference between a dyslexic brain and a non-dyslexic brain. Those with dyslexia are born with dyslexia and they will always have dyslexia. Of course, there are situations where a child not properly exposed to a literacy-rich environment could result in reading and spelling difficulties, but a good assessment will be able to determine the difference between dyslexia and poor environment.

Students with dyslexia tend to find school overwhelming, frustrating, and bewildering. They know they have the intellect but somehow they have to access the information differently. Ben Foss, author of *The Dyslexia Empowerment Plan*, states that there are three ways to learn: eye reading, ear reading, and finger reading. Those who are not dyslexic or blind can read by eye. Those who are dyslexic can "read" by ear, by listening to the content, and those who are blind read by braille (by finger). Listening to books or other print material allows students access to the content and the ability to grow their vocabularies and improve their reading skills, such as identifying main ideas and supporting details, inferencing, drawing conclusions, relating new information to background knowledge, forming opinions, etc. Just like students using eye or finger reading.

"Dyslexia is outgrown."

The fact of the matter is that a person is born with dyslexia and will always have dyslexia. They will not outgrow it, but with the correct intervention they will improve their reading and writing and can be encouraged to embrace their dyslexia. Ben Foss writes: "Welcome to the Nation of Dyslexia." He goes on to state, "Whether your child is on the cusp of being identified or you've known about his dyslexia for quite some time, I say welcome to the club! It's safe here, and you can let go of your fear and anxiety about this identification. Believe me, I know how you feel. I was there and so were my parents, and I can tell you with 100 percent certainty that it will get better. Indeed, you're going to have fun."

Holding a child with dyslexia back, and making them repeat a grade, is waiting for the child to change, when it is the intervention that needs to change. If the school is suggesting holding the child back, ask what will change to help the child be successful second time around. If you are not satisfied with their answer, perhaps holding the child back is not the answer.

"Dyslexia is an intellectual deficit."

When a child with dyslexia is struggling to read, spell, and understand or remember what she reads, it is not an intellectual deficit. In fact, in order to be diagnosed with dyslexia a child has to have a low average to above average IQ. It is common for children who are struggling to be inadvertently marginalized by the educational system because teachers (general education, special education, and reading specialists) do not know how to teach students with dyslexia because their teacher training programs did not prepare them to teach these students. The take-away here is that a child with dyslexia has as much academic potential as every other student in the classroom.

To be a really effective advocate for students with dyslexia, you must be well educated about dyslexia. I encourage you to look through the Resources section at the end of this book and read as much as you can, so that you can educate those who work with your child. In this case, knowledge really is power.

"Dyslexia requires a medical diagnosis."

No, not true at all. Dyslexia is not a medical condition. There are no medications for dyslexia and no medical interventions. In fact, usually, if you ask your pediatrician for a diagnosis they will send you to your child's school. And in many cases, if your school is misinformed, they will send you back to the pediatrician, and so goes the cycle of misinformation.

The dyslexia community is building awareness at a fast rate, and hopefully the information in this chapter will help as you move forward on your advocacy journey. It would be a good idea to make sure that you stay up to date with advances in the dyslexia community.

CHAPTER 2

Individuals with Disabilities Education Act (IDEA)—The Basics

Before we can begin to understand how to advocate for a child with dyslexia, it is important to understand the Act that protects these children. In other words, we have to understand where we have been in order to understand where we are going. The Individuals with Disabilities Education Act (IDEA) is a four-part (A–D) piece of legislation that ensures students with a disability are provided with Free Appropriate Public Education (FAPE) that is tailored to their individual needs. The IDEA (P.L. 14–149) was previously known as the Education for All Handicapped Children Act (EHA) from 1975 to 1990. In 1990 Congress reauthorized EHA and changed the title to the IDEA. Part B of the IDEA is most relevant for students with dyslexia and is composed of six main elements. These are:

(1) Individualized Education Program (IEP)

(2) FAPE

(3) Least Restrictive Environment (LRE)

(4) Appropriate Evaluation

(5) Parent and Teacher Participation, and

(6) Procedural Safeguards. The 1997 Individuals with Disabilities Education Act (IDEA) was reauthorized in 2004 under the name of Individuals with Disabilities Education Improvement Act (IDEIA) and the information in this book reflects this Act[1]. These tenets will be identified throughout the book.

Free Appropriate Public Education (FAPE)

Every child is entitled to FAPE. So what does this actually mean? The "free" in FAPE is an education that is at public expense, under public supervision and without charge. The "appropriate" in FAPE means that services must be reasonably calculated to achieve educational benefit. The "public" in FAPE means that the child will be educated in the LRE. The "education" in FAPE is the instruction and services that the child receives.

FAPE must provide education and related services that:

(A) have been provided at public expense, under public supervision and direction, and without charge

(B) meet the standards of the State educational agency

(C) include an appropriate preschool, elementary school, or secondary school education in the state involved; and

(D) are provided in conformity with the individualized education program required under section 1414(d) of this title.

United States Code, 20. Education, Section 1401 (9) (2010).

~~~~~~~~~~~~

1   The IDEIA is often still referred to as Individuals with Disabilities Act/IDEA, and these are the terms used throughout the book.

Child Find

When it comes to dyslexia, the Child Find statute is very important. Child Find requires school districts to locate and assess all students with suspected disabilities. It states, "All children with disabilities residing in the State, including children with disabilities who are homeless children or are wards of the State, and children with disabilities attending private schools, regardless of the severity of their disability, and who are in need of special education and related services, are identified, located, and evaluated" (20 USC 1412(a)(3)(A)). It is very common for students with dyslexia to be identified late and sometimes not identified at all. This can be a violation of Child Find.

Amy Rowley

Amy Rowley was a hearing impaired student in first grade. The IEP provided that Amy should be educated in a regular classroom, should continue to use the FM device, and should receive instruction from a tutor for the deaf for one hour each day and from a speech therapist for three hours each week. Amy's parents insisted that Amy also be provided with a qualified sign language interpreter in all of her academic classes in lieu of the assistance proposed in other parts of the IEP.

In 1982 *Rowley v. the Board of Education of Hendrick Hudson Central School District* was the first United States Supreme Court special education case. The Court held that FAPE requires services that provide students with "some educational benefit" (456 U.S. 176, 102 S.Ct. 3034, 73 L.Ed.2d 690). This does not require school districts to maximize the potential of children with disabilities. The Court also held that "We therefore conclude that the 'basic floor of opportunity' provided by the Act consists of access to specialized instruction and related services which are individually designed to provide educational benefit to the handicapped child." There have been some circuit court decisions that have improved on the "some educational benefit" standard, and you will need to check for these in your region.

Chevrolet or Cadillac?

In 1993 in *Doe v. the Board of Education of Tullahoma City Schools* (6th circuit) made the now famous comparison of the Chevrolet and Cadillac when it stated, "The Act requires that the Tullahoma schools provide the educational equivalent of a serviceable Chevrolet to every handicapped student. Appellant, however, demands that the Tullahoma school system provide a Cadillac solely for appellant's use. We suspect that the Chevrolet offered to appellant is in fact a much nicer model than that offered to the average Tullahoma student. Be that as it may, we hold that the Board is not required to provide a Cadillac, and that the proposed IEP is reasonably calculated to provide educational benefits to appellant, and is therefore in compliance with the requirements of the IDEA" (9 F.3d 455).

Eligibility

To qualify for special education services, the child must meet two requirements, which is the two-pronged approach to eligibility. First, the child must have a disability and show a need for services. In other words, just because a student has dyslexia (or any other disability) does not mean they automatically qualify for services. Second, it must be shown that the child needs services in order to succeed in the general education classroom.

Types of violations
PROCEDURAL VIOLATIONS

Procedural violations are those that impede the child's right to FAPE, significantly impede the parents' opportunity to participate in the decision-making process, or cause a deprivation of educational benefits. Some examples of procedural violations are:

- Not adhering to timelines.

- Incomplete IEP—not including all the elements needed in an IEP.

- Late or incomplete assessments.

- Failing to make recommendations about services clear to the parents.

- Failing to respond to the individual needs of the student.

- Predetermination of placement.

- Failing to provide procedural safeguards to the parents.

- Failing to have the required team members at meetings.

- Failing to allow parent participation.

SUBSTANTIVE VIOLATIONS

Substantive violations result in the denial of FAPE when the district does not address the student's unique needs, when the IEP is not reasonably calculated to provide some educational benefit, when the instruction and services do not happen as outlined in the IEP document, and when the placement is not in the Least Restrictive Environment (LRE). Some examples of substantive violations are:

- Failing to make recommendations based on evaluations and identified needs.

- Failing to respond to an Independant Educational Evaluation (IEE) request in a reasonable amount of time.

- Failing to write measurable goals and goals that were created to close the achievement gap.

- Failing to consider independent evaluations submitted by the parents.

- Failing to provide an intervention that responds to the child's individual needs.

- Failing to provide educational benefit to the child.

Least Restrictive Environment

Under the IDEA students are to be educated with their non-disabled peers to the maximum extent possible. A child should only be removed from regular education when his disability prevents him from being educated in the regular education classroom, even with supplementary aids and services.

Acronyms

When navigating a system like a school district you will come across acronyms and terms that will probably be new to you. This book will be more useful to you if you are familiar with the terms you will read along the way and those you may have heard in school meetings. It is important to realize that terms can vary from state to state, so if you see a term that looks as if it might be labeled something else in your district, feel free to cross it out and write in your local terminology.

ADA = Americans with Disabilities Act

AE = age equivalent

ALJ = administrative law judge

APR = Annual Performance Report

AT = assistive technology

AYP = Adequate Yearly Progress

CST = child study team

CWPM = correct words per minute

DIS = Designated Instructional Services

DOE = Department of Education

DRA = Diagnostic Reading Assessment

ESSA = Every Student Succeeds Act

ESY = Extended School Year

FAPE = Free Appropriate Public Education

fMRI = functional magnetic resonance imaging

FERPA = Family Educational Rights and Privacy Act

GE = grade equivalent

IAP = Individual Accommodation Plan (also called 504 Plan)

IDEA = Individuals with Disabilities Education Act 2004

IEE = Independent Educational Evaluation

IEP = Individualized Education Program (age 3 through 21)

ITP = Individualized Transition Plan

LD = learning disability

LEA = Local Education Agency (school district)

LEP = Limited English Proficient

LRE = Least Restrictive Environment

LSH = language, speech, and hearing

MD = multiple disabilities

MEG = Magnetoencephalography

MR = Mental Retardation (ID—Intellectual Disability)

NCLB = No Child Left Behind (federal)

NPS = Non-public school

NRP = National Reading Panel

OAH = Office of Administrative Hearings

OCR = Office of Civil Rights (federal)

OHI = other health impairment

OG = Orton-Gillingham

OT = occupational therapy

PLAAFP = Present Levels of Academic Achievement and Functional
    Performance

PLOEP = Present Levels of Educational Performance

PLOP = present levels of performance

PT = physical therapy

PWN = Prior Written Notice

QRI = Qualitative Reading Inventory

RSP = Resource Specialist Program

RtI = Response to Intervention

SAI = specialized academic instruction

SDC = Special Day Class

SEA = State Education Agency

SELPA = Special Education Local Plan Area

SpEd = Special Education

SLI = speech and language impairment

SLD = specific learning disability

SLP = speech and language pathologist

SST = student study team (also called student success team)

SWI = Structured Word Inquiry

UPL = Unlawful Practice of Law

CHAPTER 3

What to Do When You Suspect Dyslexia

Now that we have an understanding about dyslexia and some basic tenets of the Individuals with Disabilities Education Act (IDEA), let's brush up on advocating tips for students with dyslexia. Parent/guardian intuition should never be underestimated. When a parent suspects something is amiss with their child, they are usually right. Dyslexia is no exception. The main difference with dyslexia is that parents/guardians may come to this conclusion later than they would if dyslexia manifested itself physically or was otherwise obvious. Some parents eventually suspect dyslexia later in the educational process because the student with dyslexia is their first child and they have nothing to compare their child to, and often assume that the delay in reading and writing might be normal development. Some parents come to this conclusion late because they have been given the misguided, although usually well-intentioned, advice that sounds something like one or more of the following:

- Just wait another year or two, she will grow out of it.

- He is just being a boy. You know how boys are.

- It is too early to determine if dyslexia is present.

- She is fine. You're overreacting.

- She does not have dyslexia because she is receiving passing grades.

- Dyslexia is not real.

- Her reading isn't that bad. She isn't that far behind.

- We don't work with kids with dyslexia.

- She is earning As and Bs and even excelling.

- If she just repeated the grade she would catch up.

Sound familiar? Every statement above is false, and each one does nothing but delay identification and intervention. Dyslexia is not seen as a problem until it is identified, and then it becomes a disability. If a child with dyslexia is identified early, it is less likely that it will significantly impact on the student's academic life—if they receive the appropriate intervention. Many times dyslexia isn't identified until middle or high school because it is more mild to moderate and/ or it affects writing and spelling more than reading (although this could affect the reading rate).

Now that you have read the signs and symptoms in Chapter 1 you might suspect or even be convinced that the child you are advocating for is at risk of having dyslexia, or perhaps you have received an official diagnosis and would like to find out if your student is eligible for special education services. There are very specific steps you need to take. Once you read through those steps, I will guide you through what to expect from the school, and provide scenarios along the way to help you visualize the process. Each step is important no matter what the age or grade of your student. (A quick note: everything in this book is based on the IDEIA, the 2004 reauthorization of the 1997

IDEA, or Section 504 of the Rehabilitation Act 1973, but the intent of the book is to provide information that is not likely to change with new legislation. It is imperative to remember that each state is required to provide at least what is outlined in the IDEA; if a state chooses to edit their own regulations, they must only enhance the benefits. States cannot reduce the protection provided by the IDEA. Check your state educational code for laws in your area. A list of state websites is listed in Chapter 9, Resources.)

Step one: Get organized!

Document everything. And I mean *everything*. Peter Wright, a notable special education attorney and dyslexic, famously states, "If you don't document something in writing then it did not happen." Below is a list of what to document. Remember, this is just the first step in the process. Keep in mind the famous quote from Benjamin Franklin, "By failing to prepare, you are preparing to fail."

BUY A BINDER

You will need a place to store all of the information for your student's file and it needs to be big. Put everything you collect into a binder in *chronological* order with the newest on top. Put a picture of the child on the front of the binder. When you place the binder on the table with the picture prominently taking up space, it helps to remind everyone that they are talking about an individual with individual needs.

At the front of your binder should be a place where you can keep track of dates, names, contact information, and content of conversations.

Table 3.1 Communication log

Date	Relevant names	Topic	Result
09/15/2014	Mary, school psychologist	Request for testing documents prior to meeting	As of 09/22/2014, still have not received a copy of report and IEP is tomorrow.
09/22/2014	IEP team	Initial IEP and eligibility meeting	Did not receive testing reports prior to meeting, so I requested to reschedule meeting so I could have time to read the reports. Team agreed to reconvene and will send new IEP meeting notice.
09/30/2014	IEP team	New IEP meeting	I have sent emails to school psychologist and resource teacher about the date of a new meeting and have not heard back. This is now ten days past the 60 day timeline.

REQUEST EDUCATIONAL RECORD IN WRITING

Every student has an educational record that includes any and all testing, as well as report cards, health records, and screenings. The IDEA states that you should receive this within 45 days, but some states are required to get the records to you in five days or less. The educational record should also be supplied to you free of charge for the first copy.

REPORT CARDS

Keep every report card. Once you have the report cards, highlight any teacher's comments about reading and writing difficulties. See how far back those comments go.

Here is an example of a student who is in fifth grade but is reading at first grade level.

Teacher's comments over time

First grade

Zoe is a great student. She is cooperative and friendly. I enjoyed having her in my class. She needs to continue to work on sounding out words. Keep reading to her over the summer.

Second grade

Zoe had a great year. She has a lot of friends and is very helpful in the classroom. Zoe did well in math and loved to volunteer to do math problems. She needs to improve her reading and spelling. Make sure she has time to practice reading over the summer.

Third grade

Zoe continues to do well in math. When she is motivated she does well. Practice spelling and reading this summer. Use incentives to help her stay motivated.

Fourth grade

Zoe is struggling with reading and spelling, but she was a pleasure to have in class. She should continue to read this summer to help with her fluency.

Over the years there was a clear indication that Zoe was not doing well in reading and spelling while excelling in math. She did not have any behavior problems or excessive absences.

She was never assessed or referred for assessment despite the long history of an achievement gap.

~~~~~~~~~~~~~~~~~~~~~~~~~~~~

STATE AND DISTRICT TESTING

Like the report cards, find and add to your binder any and all state and district testing your student has completed. These should also be located in the educational record. Look for a pattern. Have the reading and writing scores been low for many years? Are they declining? Are they high in math and low in reading? Were accommodations used during testing? Were the assessments timed? How long did it take the student to complete the testing? How does that compare to the average student?

EMAILS

If you have ever received an email from the child's school, print it out. Additionally, create a separate file in your email inbox and store all school-related emails there. When you have a conversation with a teacher, counselor, school psychologist, principal, or administrator, follow up that conversation in writing. Remember, "If it isn't in writing, it did not happen." When sending an email, copy yourself in so that you know it went through and that the rest of the recipients are also aware that they are not the only people on the list and are paying attention to the conversation. Finally, request a simple "I received this email" from the recipients.

Here is an example of a follow-up email:

Dear Ms. Smith, Ms. Davis and Mr. Heller:

Thank you for taking the time to meet with me and my husband today (May 5, 2016) regarding our daughter, Zoe. We appreciate your time and apparent interest in helping her succeed academically. We would like to express our continued concern that Zoe is not making the academic progress that would be expected at her grade level and we believe we heard you express the same concerns. Therefore we remain in disagreement that she would not benefit from special education services and we look forward to your response to our request for an initial assessment for special education services, which we submitted at our meeting today. Please feel free to let us know if you have any questions. We look forward to a response by May 20, 2016, which is 15 days from today.

Respectfully submitted,

Kelli Sandman-Hurley

KEEP A HOMEWORK LOG

This is a great tool for those students who appear to be doing okay in the classroom but who are struggling at home. Maybe they are doing okay in the classroom because they are spending an inordinate amount of time on homework. Have you stopped fighting about homework and starting "helping" your child? Are you providing any other type of assistance to help your child with homework? Start keeping a homework log to illustrate how much time and effort your child is using to complete work that should be done in half the time. It is also helpful to document the amount and type of support you are providing. Request a copy of the school's written policy regarding homework and how much time students should be spending on it, which usually varies by grade level. School staff might dismiss the suggestion that the student is spending a lot of time on homework because they hear it so often from parents, but the homework log will provide evidence. Teachers often know that one child may spend more time than another, but they rarely understand how much time it is taking the student and how much support a parent is providing. A homework log also shows that the student isn't independent with the work. Parents want their children to do well, so they often help them with their homework, which makes it appear that the child is doing okay. This provides a false sense of the independence level of the student to the teacher and can lead the teacher to believe the student is doing okay.

The homework log can also be helpful during the discussion about accommodations for homework.

Table 3.2 A homework log

Date	Assignment	Amount of time to complete	Notes
April 1	Study for spelling test— 20 words	60 minutes	Spelled 16 words correctly on test— cannot spell the same words two weeks later.
April 3	Write a paragraph about an animal of student's choice	45 minutes	Zoe was able to dictate a coherent and grammatically sophisticated paragraph but she wrote with limited vocabulary and was obviously frustrated. She could do this independently.
April 3	Complete a sheet for 25 math facts— addition/ subtraction	Completed in ten minutes	Zoe had no trouble with this task and completed it independently.

TAKE COPIOUS NOTES AT "INFORMAL" MEETINGS

If you have any "informal" meetings with teachers and/or school administrators, follow them up with thank you emails. In these emails include the details of the meeting, who was there, and what was discussed. Usually in these meetings (sometimes called student study teams (SST) or child study teams (CST)) there will be some type of paperwork that is filled out. Keep everything and add it all to your binder.

Step two: Request an evaluation for services for a child with dyslexia

Now that you have collected data and evidence, it is time to request an assessment for special education eligibility. In a perfect world, all of the documentation above would lead to an assessment for eligibility for special education services by the school district, but we all know that we don't live in a perfect world. So you need to know what to expect, what education rights are afforded you by the 2004 IDEA, and how to prepare for any obstacles.

Prepare to become "that parent." If you make a comment to a teacher or school staff that you are going to ask for assessment for special education services, you may hear some of the following responses:

- *We don't test before third* grade—Oh yes they do! In fact, they can test as early as kindergarten. There are no federal or state regulations preventing assessment as early as kindergarten.

- *We don't test for dyslexia*—This is true. School districts do not diagnose anything. They don't diagnose ADHD, autism, dyslexia, nothing. It may seem as if they do because we tend to hear the terms autism and ADHD thrown around in meetings all the time, but they cannot diagnose those qualifying conditions either. They can only determine eligibility under specific eligibility categories. In the case of dyslexia, they will be looking at the specific learning disability (SLD) category. Interestingly, dyslexia is listed under SLD as a qualifying condition. It is important to keep in mind that just because someone has dyslexia or any other disability does not mean they automatically qualify for services. That disability must be affecting their academic performance. Here is the definition of SLD from the IDEA that you should have with you at all times. And keep copies of the statute or regulation that defines a "Specific Learning Disability" in your binder to pass out at meetings when needed. It is located in the statute at 20 USC 1401(30) and in the federal regulations at 34 CFR 300.8(c)(10):

(30) Specific learning disability

> (A) In general. The term "specific learning disability" means a disorder in one or more of the basic psychological processes involved in understanding or in using language, spoken or written, which disorder may manifest itself in the imperfect ability to listen, think, speak, read, write, spell, or do mathematical calculations.

> (B) Disorders included. Such a term includes such conditions as perceptual disabilities, brain injury, minimal brain dysfunction, *dyslexia*, and developmental aphasia.

> (C) Disorders not included. Such a term does not include a learning problem that is primarily the result of visual, hearing, or motor disabilities, of mental retardation, of emotional disturbance, or of environmental, cultural, or economic disadvantage.

Your individual state regulations may have adopted this definition. Get a copy of the definition from your state's education code so the school is aware of your state's definition (which is most likely the same).

- *We would like you to consider Response to Intervention (RtI) instead of an assessment*—A school cannot deny an assessment in order to try RtI. See the memo from the United States Department of Education Office of Special Education and Rehabilitive Services (for details, go to "Websites" in the References section at the end of the book).

What is RtI anyway?

RtI is a multitiered approach to help struggling learners. In this model, it is meant to be proactive, and students' progress is monitored as they move through different stages (usually three tiers) of the intervention to determine the need for further research-based instruction and/or intervention:

- ~ *Tier 1 Core Instruction:* This stage takes place in the general education classroom where the teacher differentiates instruction that research has shown is effective.

- ~ *Tier 2 Group Interventions:* If the child is not making adequate progress in Tier 1 she will begin receiving intervention in small groups.

- ~ *Tier 3 Intensive Interventions:* If the child is not making adequate progress in Tier 2 she will begin receiving more intensive intervention.

The RtI model can be problematic for students with dyslexia in that the research-based interventions that are chosen might not be appropriate and valuable time can be lost. Additionally, general education teachers are usually not sufficiently trained to implement programs that are appropriate for students with dyslexia. Finally, if a child is showing progress in a tier they may be determined to be a success story and taken out of RtI before real mastery has taken place.

~~~~~~

- *Spelling is not a big deal*—This is up for debate, but I believe spelling is of the utmost importance. Think about this for a minute. If a student can read a word it does not mean they can spell it, but if a student can spell a word, they will be able to read it. If a child can spell a word, that is evidence that they truly understand the structure of English. Some adults with dyslexia will tell you that they are still horrible spellers and that it doesn't affect them at all. Others will tell you it is horribly embarrassing. So, yes, it is important, and technology is not the answer—a deep understanding of our language, which should be a human right, is the answer. The real issue lies in the fact that most educators have not been trained in this structure themselves, so it goes untaught or taught via rote memorization techniques. It is common to hear from middle and high school staff that they do not teach spelling, which is not accurate. When you are told that nothing can be done due to school policy, politely request the written policy regarding this statement.

- *We would like you to attend an "informal" meeting*—This is a time-waster. A stalling tactic. A filler. Politely decline and move forward with the written request. If the school staff state they are following school protocol or policy, ask for the policy in writing. The policy cannot conflict with regulations that once you have put a request in writing they have 15 days to respond to your request. The clock is still ticking on any timelines that have been set in to motion for previous requests, regardless of this meeting. If you do decide to attend this meeting, politely make sure you remind them that your written request is still pending.

A NOTE TO HOMESCHOOLERS AND STUDENTS IN PRIVATE SCHOOLS

If a student who is homeschooled is suspected of having dyslexia, have them assessed for special education services by your local (home) school district. The same rules apply to this assessment as they do to students who are enrolled and attending the local school. The IDEA has left it up to the individual states to decide if they will also offer services to the homeschooled student if they are found to be eligible for special education services. You will need to check with your local district to find out what their policies are regarding homeschooled and private schooled students.

WHAT THE ASSESSMENT REQUEST SHOULD INCLUDE

In order to have a student assessed for eligibility for special education services, the parents or guardians need to write a compelling letter (see Section 614 Evaluations, eligibility determinations, Individualized Education Programs, and educational placements) requesting the assessment. In this letter you must describe the difficulty your child is having and how it is affecting their academic success. Include how much time they spend on homework and how long they study for tests and quizzes. Describe their early experiences with reading. Were they resistant to reading as a preschooler? Were they slow to learn the alphabet? Is their spelling below their reading level? Are they frustrated by reading? Is there a family history of reading and writing difficulties? Write the letter as if the people who read the letter have never met your child. Below is an example of a letter requesting an assessment for a child with dyslexia.

> Date
>
> School name
> Principal
> School address
>
> RE: (student's name)
>
> Dear (Principal or Special Education Director),
>
> I am writing in regard to my daughter (add student's name), who is (insert # years) years old and in (insert teacher's name and grade level) grade class, to request an initial assessment to determine eligibility for special education services according to the provisions set forth in the Individuals with Disabilities Education Act (IDEA 2004).
>
> My husband/wife (or appropriate person/people) and I are quite concerned that (student's name) has a learning disability that is affecting her learning and school performance. She is a very charming, gregarious and smart little girl but is struggling with her academics. I am requesting a full evaluation in all areas of suspected disability for the following reasons:
>
> - (student's name) is smart and capable of learning; however, she is having great difficulty with her grade level reading and spelling. In fact, I believe my child is about two grade levels behind her peers.
>
> - She is able to complete class work and homework, but it takes her longer than most of her peers. She sometimes needs directions read to her so she can complete the task. I have observed this in her class and at home.

- Her reading and spelling scores at the first reporting period were far below average. Her scores for reading were below basic. (Teacher's name) indicated that her performance on the testing did not show much increase in the area of reading.

- On her first trimester progress report she was working below standard or progressing toward standard in most areas. See attached copy of her first progress report.

- She is currently too far behind in the targeted level of reading for her to be on track to prepare for second grade. Please see attached reading comprehension sample.

- She continues to struggle with spelling and writing. Please see attached writing samples.

- She continues to struggle in math. (If possible, insert a concrete example such as: It takes her so long to complete her workbook pages that she never has time to get to her additional math packet. She has yet to complete many pages of the first packet and many of her class members have already handed it in.)

- She is very capable of learning, but it takes a lot more repetition, practice and processing time than her peers. This has been observed by me, my husband/wife, other family members, (teacher's name) and (insert any additional school staff who may have input).

- In several discussions I have had with (teacher's name), she has expressed great concern for (student's name) and her ongoing struggles. She has expressed that (student's name) tries very hard during class, but she is not at grade level expectations. I know you will speak with (teacher's name) about her observations and concerns.

- We support (student's name) education by spending a lot of time on homework and extra instructional practice at home in reading, spelling, writing, and math. We spend much more time than the expected (insert the amount of time based on grade level. Example: 20–30 minutes for a first grader) to complete homework. We are aware of the importance of the support we need to provide at home, including providing guidance to complete homework, reading at least 20 minutes every day, practicing on educational websites, incorporating reading, spelling and math practice in our everyday environment and tasks, etc. However, (student's name) continues to struggle. We will continue to provide support at home, but (student's name) needs additional support during school hours to help her be successful at learning (insert grade level) grade content.

I thank you for the time you will take to consider the needs of (student's name) and I look forward to working with you and the school staff over the next 15 days[1] to develop an effective assessment plan for her. I would be happy to discuss any questions you may have regarding the above or to supply additional information, so please do not hesitate to contact me. You can contact me by phone at any time. I am also on campus every morning, at the end of the regular school day, and volunteer at various times, so please feel free to ask me to meet at any time.

Sincerely,

(Parent's name)

cc: child's teacher and any other appropriate staff

---

1   Always remember to check your state laws about timelines.

Once you have written this letter, you have several different ways to make sure it is delivered. You can submit it via email, while copying yourself in on that email, snail mail with delivery confirmation, or hand-deliver your letter (make sure to get it date-stamped and ask for a copy)—or you can do all three. Once the school receives the letter they have 15 calendar (or business) days to respond to you in writing (but check local state laws). If there is a school break during this time that is more than five days, those days are not counted, and this is referred to as a tolling period. Remember to record the date you sent this letter in your binder. If you send a request in the last week of school, those last days count, so do not let the school tell you to wait until the fall.

The district is required to respond to your written request *in writing* (Section 300.503 Prior written notice) within 15 calendar days (but check local state laws). If they do not respond within a reasonable time, this could potentially mean they denied FAPE because they delayed the assessment process which delayed an offer of appropriate services, and this might be a procedural violation. This is a good place to remember to choose your battles carefully. Ask yourself if it is worth battling over a timeline. In some cases it will be, and in others it will not.

Step three: The district response to your letter requesting assessment
PRIOR WRITTEN NOTICE (PWN)

This is the notice you will receive from the school district in response to your written request for assessment for special education services. PWN must be sent if the school is proposing to do any of the following things (Section 300.503(a)):

- initiate or change the identification, evaluation, or educational placement of your child

- initiate or change the provision of FAPE to your child

- refuse to initiate or change the identification, evaluation, or educational placement of your child

- refuse to initiate or change the provision of FAPE to your child.

If the school denies the assessment they are required to outline why they denied it. The PWN should include:

- a description of the action proposed or refused by the school

- an explanation of why the school proposes or refuses to take the action

- a description of each evaluation procedure, assessment, record, or report the school used as a basis for their decision

- a statement that the parents of a child with a disability have protection under the procedural safeguards and how the parents can obtain a copy of them

- sources for parents to contact to obtain assistance in understanding these provisions

- a description of other options that the Individualized Education Team (IEP) team considered, and the reasons why those options were rejected

- a description of other factors relevant to the school's proposal or refusal (Section 300.503(b) Prior notice).

Additionally, if the PWN of denial states that they want to try RtI *before* the assessment, then you can remind them that according to the memo from the Office of Special Education and Rehabilitative Services written on January 21, 2011, the school district is prohibited from denying assessments based on RtI (see the "Websites" section in the References).

If the school agrees to the assessment to determine eligibility for special education services, you will receive an *assessment plan*. You then have 15 days (check your local state laws about timelines) to respond and agree to the assessment plan. You can take longer than 15 days, but that will delay the assessment. For a child with dyslexia there is a possibility that there are some co-existing (often referred to as co-morbid) conditions, and the school is responsible for assessing all areas related to the suspected disability (Section 300.304(c)(4)). You usually have the following assessment options:

Academic—In the case of a student with dyslexia, this is the battery of tests that will be the most helpful. So make sure this box is checked. Feel free to ask the school what battery of tests will be used and who will be assessing the student. We will get to the interpretation of the testing later. Below is a list of tests that are commonly used to determine if a student is having difficulty with reading and spelling. You can request particular assessments, but it is important to remember that school districts have the right to choose the assessments they use during the assessment process:

Comprehensive Test of Phonological Processing-2 (CTOPP-2)

Gray Oral Reading Test-5 (GORT-5)

Test of Word Reading Efficiency-2 (TOWRE-2)

Woodcock-Johnson IV Tests of Achievement® (WJ-IV®)

Test of Written Language—Fourth Edition (TOWL-4)

Gray Silent Reading Tests (GSRT)

Test of Auditory Processing (TAPS-3)

Test of Written Spelling (TWS-5)

Wechsler Individual Achievement Test® (WIAT III®)

Nelson-Denny Reading Test™

Spelling Assessment—This deserves its own paragraph because spelling tends to be woefully misunderstood and virtually ignored in IEP meetings. In fact, I have heard on numerous occasions that spelling doesn't matter, isn't important or isn't taught. And while I find these comments intriguing in that they shine a light on an area of education that needs some improvement, we are talking about spelling assessment here. Spelling assessments can vary from a subtest on the WJ-IV® to a good analysis with an informal assessment like the spelling chart in the *Words Their Way: Teacher's Manual*. A subtest like the WJ-IV® will give you a standard score, percentile, grade equivalent, and age equivalent, but a spelling survey will speak volumes about what a child understands and what she does not understand about English orthography. The table below shows an example of what misspellings can tell the IEP team about the needs of a student with dyslexia (and this applies to students without dyslexia as well).

Table 3.3 Spelling analysis

Word	Student's spelling	Analysis	Instructional needs
been	ben	Student has difficulty remembering sight words. Student also does not understand that <been> is be + en —> been	Instruction in sight words, morphology, and etymology.
have	hav	Student has difficulty remembering sight words. Student also does not know the English convention that words will not end in <v>.	Instruction in sight words and basic English spelling conventions.

every	evry	This student does not understand that spoken syllables don't always match written syllables. Also has a mistaken notion that there is a direct sound-symbol correlation between spoken words and written words.	Instruction in understanding that the meaning of words sometimes supersedes the phonology. Also, needs instruction in the role of the schwa in English.[2]
health	helth	This student is spelling based on a strict sound–symbol relationship. The student is also having difficulty remembering health is heal + th —> health.	Instruction in understanding that the meaning of words sometimes supersedes the phonology. Also, build an understanding that sometimes pronunciation shifts but spelling does not.

Cognitive—In the case of students with dyslexia, an assessment of cognitive ability will also be included in the assessment plan. If a previous and recent cognitive assessment was conducted elsewhere, the school may opt to use the previous information. This should be administered and interpreted only by the school psychologist. The most common cognitive assessments are the Wechsler Intelligence

2   Words with schwas and unaccented syllables tend to get dropped, or elided, in English. Therefore it is important for a student to understand that the second syllable in <every> is pronounced in the base word <ever> in order to understand the spelling.

Scale for Children® (WISC-V®) or the Kaufman Assessment Battery for Children (KABC). For children who are 16–19 years old the Wechsler Adult Intelligence Scale—Fourth Edition® (WAIS-IV®) is usually administered. This testing is done to determine if the student has the intellectual capacity to learn and to identify the student's strength and weaknesses.

Speech and language—Many students with dyslexia also have speech issues. It is important to remember that speech is not only about articulation, but a student may have difficulty with expressive or receptive language, and this is something that needs to be evaluated by a speech and language pathologist (SLP). If you suspect this is also an area of concern, then you can request to have the district test for this.

Occupational therapy (OT)—Some students with dyslexia can also have symptoms of dysgraphia. They may have difficulty with the physical act of writing and getting their thoughts down on paper. Students with dysgraphia will grip their writing utensils tightly and awkwardly. Their spelling suffers and their handwriting might border on illegible. If this is an area of concern then you can ask for an OT assessment to determine if services are needed to improve fine motor skills.

Whether or not OT services will help a child with dysgraphia is up for debate, but it is important to understand what dysgraphia is. Below is the definition from the International Dyslexia Association (IDA):

> dysgraphia is the condition of impaired letter writing by hand, that is, disabled handwriting. Impaired handwriting can interfere with learning to spell words in writing and speed of writing text. Children with dysgraphia may have only impaired handwriting, only impaired spelling (without reading problems), or both impaired handwriting and impaired spelling.

Physical therapy (PT)—In the case of dyslexia, physical therapy is usually not an area of concern. But if you believe your student also needs some assistance with mobility and large motor skills, then you can request a PT assessment.

Social/emotional—This is a very underutilized area of assessment for students with dyslexia and the need can be obvious, especially for older students. If a student has continued to fail, fall behind or struggle through school despite motivation, intellectual ability, and home and school support, there is a good chance their self-esteem is going to suffer. This can affect their attitude toward school and can be related to the suspected disability. If you believe your student is socially or emotionally affected by their dyslexia, you can check this box too.

Assistive technology (AT)—We are in an age where technology is our friend but not our teacher. For a student with dyslexia, technology can be their key to accessing the grade level content they are capable of learning in a format other than print. Every child who is assessed for special education services under the SLD category should also be assessed for AT. This means that an AT specialist will meet with the student and determine which devices and/or programs would be the best accommodations for the student (Section 300.6(a) Assistive technology service). On request, parents and students are also eligible for training in the AT they are being offered.

A WORD ABOUT TESTING SPECIFICALLY FOR DYSLEXIA

If I have heard it once, I have heard it a million times, "Our school does not test for dyslexia." Yes, that is true; they do not—in most states (check your state for current laws regarding dyslexia). What they do test for is a specific learning disability because that is the eligibility category where dyslexia is listed as one of the qualifying conditions. So, when you request an assessment from the school, arguing over the terminology at this early stage is not important. It will become important later in the process, unless your state has a law specifically addressing the identification of dyslexia. I will revisit this when we get to the initial IEP meeting. However, the Office of Special Education and Rehabilitative Services released a Dyslexia Guidance memo in October 2015 reminding school districts that they are not prohibited from using the word dyslexia or including dyslexia and appropriate methodology in IEP documents. (See the "Websites" section in References at the end of the book).

Step four: Assessment conducted and initial IEP meeting convened

Once you have agreed to the assessment plan most states will have 60 calendar days (check your state laws) (Section 300.301(c)(1) Initial Evaluations) to conduct the initial battery of assessments to determine eligibility and hold the initial IEP meeting. During this time your student will meet with a school psychologist and special education teacher as well as anyone assessing for related services (OT, SLP) who may be conducting testing. Keep an eye on how often this is happening and how long they are keeping your student during these sessions. It is not uncommon to do a lot of assessments towards the deadline date.

SCENARIO: THE SCHOOL IS NOT ALLOWED TO CONDUCT TESTING FOR SPECIAL EDUCATION SERVICE

If assessment is denied you do have some recourse. Remember to revisit the PWN to determine if the notice includes all the information that is required in a denial notice. You can gather more information for the school to consider, and then resubmit your request. That additional information might include:

- reading fluency rates

- spelling samples

- a homework log to show how long it takes the student to complete common tasks.

At this point you can also consider obtaining a private assessment and submitting that report to the school for reconsideration of their initial denial. The school can then decide to assess the student or they can deny the assessment again. If you receive another denial, you might consider consulting an attorney for the next steps.

If your student is assessed but is then denied services because they are gifted, or they didn't meet a state-mandated cut-off score, Read the memo entitled "Letter to Jim Delisle" written by the Office of Special Education and Rehabilative Services on December 20, 2013 which stated, in part:

> it would be inconsistent with the IDEA for a child, regardless of whether the child is gifted, to be found ineligible for special education and related services under the SLD category solely because the child scored above a particular cut score established by State policy. Further, under 34 CFR 300.309(a)(1), the group described in 300.306 may determine that a child has an SLD if the child 'does not achieve adequately for the child's age or to meet State-approved grade level standards...when provided with learning experiences and instruction appropriate for the child's age or State-approved grade level standards' in one or more of the following areas: oral expression; listening comprehension; written expression; basic reading skill; reading fluency skills; reading comprehension; mathematics calculation; or mathematics problem solving.

You have now done all the work to get an assessment completed and are ready to attend the IEP meeting.

CHAPTER 4

The IEP Meeting

"He who fails to prepare, prepares to fail."

BENJAMIN FRANKLIN

Congratulations! The school agreed to assess your child to determine if he is eligible for special education services, and you most likely had to wait the entire 60 days (check your local state laws) for the initial Individualized Education Program (IEP) meeting. Now the hard part starts. You need to be *very prepared* for the next steps in the process, because you might run into obstacles.

Preparing for the initial IEP

To this day, I still have nervous energy before an IEP meeting. IEP meetings can be intimidating and frustrating. Many times you just don't know what you are going to encounter during this meeting, so you need to prepare and prepare well.

Request assessments prior to the IEP meeting: First, you can request the assessment reports prior to the meeting and you should receive these 24–48 hours in advance so that you have the chance to be prepared. If you do not receive them before the meeting, you can request that the first meeting be used to review the assessments and schedule a second IEP meeting to create the IEP – if an IEP is to be created. If you do not receive the assessments prior to the meeting, you can accept the assessments at the meeting and tell the team you would like to review them and reschedule a new meeting. It is your right to have the opportunity to review the assessments outside the IEP meeting (Section 300.613). The Family Educational Rights and Privacy Act (FERPA) requires that "educational agencies and institutions comply with a request by a parent or eligible student for access to education records within a reasonable period of time, but not more than 45 days after receipt of a request. Some States have laws that may require that parents and eligible students be granted access in a shorter time period."

Audio recording meetings: From this point on, you can tell the IEP team that you will be audio recording each and every meeting that you have with the school. In many states you need to give at least 24-hours' notice (check local state laws) that you are going to record the meeting so that they can do the same. In other states, the Individuals with Disabilities Education Act (IDEA) has left it up to districts to determine the notification timeline and sometimes no notice is required at all. For a complete explanation about audio recording, the Office of Special Education has produced a clarification letter on its website (see the References section at the end of the book). However, you can remind the IEP team that the policy is required to include exceptions to ensure parents understand the IEP. You cannot be denied the option to record a meeting just because the team does not want to be recorded, but whatever you do, do not record secretly. Do not feel as though this is an aggressive move on your part or that you are setting a negative tone from the beginning. This is just another way to keep records. You may also want to record it because your spouse or another significant member of your team was not able to make it to the meeting. Perhaps you want to make sure you heard everything and would like the tapes to go back and review all the information that was given to you at this meeting. When nerves kick in, retention can leave the building, and who understands that better than educators?

The initial IEP meeting—it's your party and you can cry if you want to

The initial IEP meeting can be one of the most intimidating and overwhelming experiences of your life, especially if you do not know what to expect. Imagine walking into a room with ten to fifteen education professionals, all ready to talk about your student. If you are not prepared for that scenario, it can be an unnerving experience. As well as you, members of the team will include those who have conducted an assessment or someone qualified to interpret the assessment results, the general education teacher(s), special education teacher, and "a representative of the local education agency (LEA) who is: qualified to provide, or supervise the provision of, specially designed instruction to meet the unique needs of children with disabilities; knowledgeable about the general education curriculum; and knowledgeable about the availability of resources of the LEA" (Section 300.321 IEP Team). It is also very likely that the IEP team had a meeting before you arrived to make sure they are all on the same page. This usually becomes obvious quickly.

If you are a parent try not to go to a meeting alone. If you can, take a friend, family member, or advocate. If you are not able to take someone with you, find someone you can text or call during the meeting. You can also have someone join via phone or teleconferencing (Skype, Facetime, Zoom, etc.). Before the meeting begins you might want to ask who is representing the district and if that person has the necessary qualifications as listed above. You are also allowed to take breaks during the meeting to step outside and make a call, take a deep breath, or cry. Don't forget that you can always request a part two or three or four of a meeting. There is no regulation or statute that states a meeting has to be completed in one day, but remember to be reasonable. During the meeting, make sure you ask any and all clarifying questions you need so that you are completely informed about what the team is talking about and you can make sensible contributions and decisions. However, keep in mind that the services will not begin until the IEP is signed.

EXPECT TO BE OVERWHELMED WITH INFORMATION ABOUT YOUR CHILD

People always ask me if I ever focus on the strengths of the student I am advocating for, and they say it with a tinge of annoyance that I seem to focus on the negative. Well, here's the thing, I am in an IEP meeting advocating for the appropriate services for a student who is struggling. Time is of the essence in most of these meetings, so no, I don't focus on the strengths as much as I do the weaknesses. I am focusing on the weaknesses because I am trying to make them strengths.

The IEP can be difficult for parents because they have to sit and listen to several people talk about the strengths and weaknesses of their child. Although there will be plenty of strengths, the focus of the initial meeting is to determine eligibility, if the child requires special education services, and if the child requires related services. If this is not the initial meeting then the focus will be on progress and current level of services. This is the time to remember that if you are the parent, you know your child better than anyone else in that room. Don't be afraid to let the team know when you disagree with their statements about your child. However, it is equally important to remember that the school staff may see things at school that you do not see at home, so try to be open to their observations as well. Sometimes behaviors at home are different from behaviors at school and it is important to remember that. You, the parent/guardian, are an equal member of the IEP team and your input must be considered and documented. Depending on the age of your child, you might consider having the child come to the IEP meeting. This is recommended in middle school and beyond. The child might even come to the beginning of the meeting to give their own statement about their IEP or their school experience. It also gives them the opportunity to advocate for themselves and take ownership of their plan. If the child is too young or does not want to attend, then consider having them record a statement and play it at the meeting. Also, consider recording your child reading something at grade level to play for the IEP team if necessary, or bring a writing sample of something they produced independently. Remember, this is all part of the child's educational record, so you need to get the record straight from the beginning. At some point in the meeting, ideally at the beginning, ask the team if you can read a statement that describes how dyslexia has impacted on your student, your student's family, and their learning and educational progress as well as on achieving state standards. This is not the time to point fingers or make accusations.

You are part of the IEP team and you are part of the decision-making process.

Student self-advocacy

Jake was in the fifth grade when I met him. He had been struggling in school since first grade. He had yearly IEPs but never seemed to make any progress, despite being bright and attentive with parents who were advocating for him each year. When he transitioned to middle school his behavior really started to deteriorate, so we went to observe him during his time receiving special education services and his time in general education. What became instantly obvious was that although he was not able to read and spell like his peers, he was bored to tears in his resource classes because he wasn't learning the content his peers were learning. On top of that, he was grouped inappropriately with classmates with significantly different needs. So,

Jake self-advocated and asked if he could attend a regular English class, and lo and behold, he loved it. He was excited about the topic and described everything that had occurred during the class he observed. When the next IEP meeting came up Jake asked if he could attend and his parents excitedly agreed. The IEP meeting consisted of no less than ten adults, who were there to talk about Jake as he sat and politely (maybe with an eye roll here and there) listened. At the end he successfully advocated his way out of the resource room (he was receiving more one-on-one instruction outside school) and into an honors English class. We made sure that he knew he would only be successful if he used the accommodations that were put in place for him (he was significantly behind in reading and writing) and he had to agree before the move was made. Jake successfully completed that course and remained in general education English classes with much improved behavior.

The lesson here is that it can be extremely beneficial to have the student advocate for themselves at these meetings. It gives them power over their own education and it also makes them responsible for their choices. Of course, not all students will be comfortable speaking to ten adults like Jake did, but I think given the opportunity they might surprise us.

The disappearing IEP team

All required members of the student's IEP team should be present at the meeting. However, it is not uncommon to be asked if the general education teacher, or any other member, can be excused from attending. There might be some circumstances where this would be okay, but when we are talking about a child who has dyslexia and is struggling with reading and writing, it is imperative to have the general education teacher present. If you decide that it is okay for this teacher, or any other team member, not to attend the meeting, sign a release (Section 300.321 IEP Team) and the teacher should submit a written report regarding their observations of your child, progress reports, and any other pertinent information. This is not ideal, as teachers should be part of the entire IEP process. This should happen prior to the meeting so you have the opportunity to reschedule. You can also reschedule the meeting right then and there if the appropriate members are not present.

It is also not uncommon to have teachers and other IEP team members ask to be excused when they have finished giving their input. This is totally up to you. If you are satisfied with their participation and you have asked all the questions you need to, then by all means, let them go on about their day. However, if you think they might have some valuable input into other parts of the meeting, then politely request that they stay.

In the case of middle and high school students, every teacher who works with your student needs to attend the IEP meeting. It is tempting to let the PE teacher and the art teacher off the hook, but they may have something very valuable to add that you didn't even think about. At least get a written statement from them.

On more occasions than I would like to admit, I have noticed that the "administrative representative" at the meeting does not really qualify as such.

How to read the reports

Once the meeting begins there may be an agenda that is shared and agreed on. At initial eligibility meetings it is common to begin with a review of the assessments. For annual IEP meetings, the progress on goals is usually the starting point. Then the team reviews current present levels (see page 111), which provides the information you need for the goals. Remember, needs drive goals and goals drive services. As you listen to the assessment results remember that the team cannot rely on one test, one test score or one piece of information. The IDEA requires that the testing includes: a variety of assessment tools and strategies to gather relevant functional, developmental, and academic information about the child, including information provided by the parent, that may assist in determining eligibility (Section 300.304(b) (1) Evaluation procedures). To make sure that you are able to make decisions in response to several pieces of information, it is vital to learn how to read and understand the reports. In this chapter I provide a quick description of how to interpret the scores, but keep in mind that standard scores (discussed next) and reading fluency measures alone are not enough to identify all areas of suspected disability, and if there is evidence that dyslexia or a specific learning disability (SLD) is present (Section 300.307(a) Specific learning disabilities). IEP teams should also consider information including teacher reports, parent reports, outside tutoring reports, outside assessments, report cards, observations, district and state testing, writing samples, etc. Note that the IDEA does not require the determination of eligibility to be based on discrepancy only.

In 1977 the discrepancy model was introduced which required that a student needed to have "a severe discrepancy between achievement and intellectual ability in one or more of the areas: (1) oral expression; (2) listening comprehension; (3) written expression; (4) basic reading skill; (5) reading comprehension; (6) mathematics calculation; or (7) mathematic reasoning" (United States Office of Education 1977). In 2004 the following language was added to the IDEA: "when determining whether a child has a specific learning disability, as defined in Section 1401 of this title, a local educational agency shall not be required to take into consideration whether a child has a severe discrepancy between achievement and intellectual ability" (Section 1414(b)(6)(A)). IEP teams can no longer determine eligibility based on discrepancy alone.

If you have an outside assessment, either paid for privately or completed through an Independant Educational Evaluation (IEE) (discussed later in this chapter), the school must consider the outside assessment, but they do not have to agree with the results. It is important to ask the school staff what they agree and disagree with and why. This information needs to be in writing or recorded so that their reasoning is documented.

Imagine this scenario in a meeting: you're handed the testing and the IEP and as you flip through it, you notice that it states, "child does not qualify for services at this time."

This is just flat-out not okay. Any predetermination of services or eligibility is eliminating the parent participation that is imperative, and this is not allowed by the IDEA. There can be preplanning but not predetermination, and if the school seems unwilling to listen to ideas alternative to theirs, then predetermination may be in effect. Any eligibility determination is to be made by the team, and that cannot happen without parent input, because the parent is part of the team. When this happens, kindly remind the team that there is supposed be a discussion regarding qualification, and any predetermination is contradictory to the IDEA regulations regarding participation. But beware of a superficial effort by the IEP team to include you. If you do not feel as if your opinions are really being considered, do not sign the IEP, and if the IEP has a line that says "parents were given the opportunity to participate," do not sign it.

Assessment jargon

So there you are, sitting at a table with no less than seven "experts." Each one takes a turn talking about your beloved child. Your baby. The peanut butter to your jelly. The reason you wake up every morning. As they talk they rattle off numbers, names of tests, names of programs, and percentages, and they bust out charts that are supposed to make this all make sense to you. If this phase of the process leaves you feeling as if you are listening to Charlie Brown, then you need to read on!

Statistics can be intimidating and confusing. In fact, in my sophomore year of college at the University of Arizona, my statistics professor walked into the classroom the first day of class with a chainsaw. That's right, a chainsaw. He fired up that chainsaw and announced that we were going to annihilate statistics. If I understood his point (and perhaps I am way off) he knew we were all a little worried about his class and we had heard the rumors about how impossible statistics were, so he was trying to break the tension. I will never forget him because he gave me the confidence that I could understand it.

The Bell Curve

In most initial IEP meetings, and the triennials that follow, many parents will be presented with a picture of the Bell Curve with numbers and lines drawn on it in an attempt to explain where the student is in comparison to their same age and/or grade peers. Sometimes it will be used as a visual to show that there is not a discrepancy, or a "big enough" discrepancy, but you now know that a discrepancy alone is not enough to determine eligibility. However, the Bell Curve can be an interesting way to visually demonstrate strengths, weaknesses, and current areas of needed improvement, and how they compare to your child's peers.

THE BELL CURVE: HOW IQ SCORES ARE DISTRIBUTED ACROSS GROUPS OF PEOPLE

The Bell Curve has a peak in the middle and two tails at either end. Most scores fall in the middle of the graph, which creates the shape of a bell, and these scores are considered average. When scores fall in the right-hand side of the tail, the scores are considered above average to superior. When the scores fall in the left-hand side of the tail, the scores are considered below average.

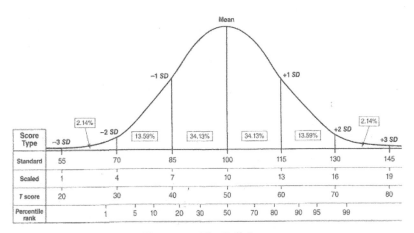

Figure 4.1 The Bell Curve

When using the Bell Curve you need to know what the mean is, what standard deviations are, and how they are interpreted. The mean is the middle of the curve, the 50th percentile. For most educational assessments the average mean score is the standard score of 100 and a subtest score or scaled score of ten.

The standard deviation (SD) is how to determine how far from the mean a score falls. One SD is 15 points. If the score is 0 SD from the mean, then the score is at 100 or the 50th percentile. If the score falls one SD below the mean, the score is 85, which is the 16th percentile. If the score falls one SD above the mean, the scores is 115, which is the 84th percentile. If the score falls two SDs below the mean, the score will be 70 and that is in the poor range. If the score falls two SDs above the mean, the score is 130 and is in the superior range. Most scores will fall somewhere between the 85th and 16th percentiles, which usually constitutes the average range. This is equivalent to where 68 percent of the general population will score.

For children with dyslexia, the Bell Curve is often used to show the IQ score in comparison with the academic achievement scores, and this is where graphs and visuals can be deceiving. Figure 4.1 illustrates the case of a student with average IQ and low average academic skills. If the team is going solely on this data it looks as if the student is doing "fine," but you need to ask some questions to add more information to this simplistic view of dyslexia and academic achievement.

Raw scores

I am not going to give much attention to raw scores because they are pretty meaningless in the context of special education and standardized assessments. But nonetheless, you should know what a raw score is. If you take a test that has 90 questions and you answer 77 of the questions correctly, then your raw score is 77. Raw scores will be revisited again in the criterion-referenced assessments section on page 83.

Standard scores (SS)

Standard scores (SS) are the lifeblood of IEP meetings and are a large part of the determination of eligibility and progress. The assessor takes the raw score and, using the assessment handbook, he converts it into the SS, and now we have something we can work with. The SS is what the team will use to determine how the student is performing based on a comparison of a large group (sample) of same-aged and/or grade peers. The average range can be anywhere from 85 to 115 depending on the assessment, but this range can vary. So, be very astute when reading through these scores. On many occasions I have seen the Comprehensive Test of Phonological Processing-2 (CTOPP-2) scores reported as average when the standard score is 82 and on the CTOPP-2 this is actually below average, but on the IV Tests of Achievement® (WJ-IV®) it is low average. If you are not sure, ask for clarification on what the ranges are for each test they are presenting, and request to see the testing manual.

Percentiles

Percentiles are often reported, but should be considered only for information and not something to hang your hat on. But this is how they are read: if a student has a standard score of 100, then you have a percentile of 50. This means that the student scored the same or better than 50 percent of his peers. If the student has a standard score of 90, then you have a percentile of 25. This means that the student scored the same or better then 25 percent of his peers.

Intelligence scores

An intelligence quotient, or IQ score, is a number used to describe a person's current cognitive abilities. We call an IQ score of 100 the mean, or average score. In special education the areas of cognition that are assessed are verbal ability, non-verbal ability, processing speed, and working memory. On the most popular cognitive assessment, the Wechsler Intelligence Scale for Children® (WISC-IV®), the score in each area will indicate ability in the various areas described below:

VERBAL COMPREHENSION

Similarities—Items requiring the child to describe how two given things are alike. This measures the child's skill in comparative reasoning.

Vocabulary—Words of increasing difficulty are presented orally and visually. The child is required to define the words. This measures verbal knowledge and concept formation.

PERCEPTUAL REASONING

Block design—Children put together red-and-white blocks in a pattern according to a displayed model. This is timed, and some of the more difficult puzzles award bonuses for speed.

Picture concepts—Children are provided with a series of pictures presented in rows (either two or three rows) and asked to determine which pictures go together, one from each row.

Matrix reasoning—Children are shown an array of pictures with one missing square, and select the picture that fits the array from five options.

THE WORKING MEMORY INDEX'S (WMI'S) SUBTESTS

Digit span—children are orally given sequences of numbers and asked to repeat them, either as heard or in reverse order.

Letter-number sequencing—children are provided with a series of numbers and letters and asked to provide them back to the examiner in a predetermined order.

THE PROCESSING SPEED INDEX'S (PSI'S) SUBTESTS

Coding—Children under eight mark rows of shapes with different lines according to a code; children over eight transcribe a digit-symbol code. The task is time-limited, with bonuses for speed.

Symbol search—Children are given rows of symbols and target symbols and asked to mark whether or not the target symbols appear in each row.

Standard scores have a mean (average) of 100. Scores from about 90 to 110 are considered average. Some assessment SS labels will vary, meaning that an SS of 85 might be considered low average on one test and below average on another.

Age and grade equivalents

Grade equivalents are reported as GE 3.5, which means a grade equivalent of third grade and fifth month. Age equivalents (AE) are reported as AE 6.6, which means an age equivalent of six years and six months old.

On the surface it looks as if this information would be an easy way to describe the student's current levels and progress, but there are just too many variables that go into this measurement to make it a sufficient stand-alone piece of information.

These scores are especially unhelpful in the case of students with dyslexia because it is impossible to account for the variability of what is taught in one grade level and another. In addition, many students with dyslexia have been held back at some point in their education careers. These scores should not be used to determine eligibility or progress.

Subtest scores

Most assessments consist of short individual tests that assess particular skills and these are called subtests. Although the exact testing protocol varies from assessment to assessment, some examples of subtests are:

Word attack—This assesses the child's ability to read words in isolation. These tests usually include real words and non-words.

Reading fluency—This type of assessment measures how quickly and accurately the child can read a passage or sentence. This is usually a time assessment.

Calculation—This usually assesses how well, and sometime how quickly, the child can complete simple calculation problems.

Spelling—This usually assesses spelling by dictating words in isolation.

Writing—This usually assesses the child's ability to write and put sentences together, and his written organization. It does not mark down for spelling.

Passage comprehension—This usually assesses the child's ability to understand what they read.

Oral comprehension—This usually assesses the child's ability to understand passages that are read to them. This subtest removes the print aspect of literacy.

Most assessments will combine a set of subtest scores and calculate a composite score for a general skill set like basic reading skills (discussed in the next section). Be sure to ask for the subtest scores if they are not provided on your report. These scores can be very important in looking for specific areas of weakness.

What is often not reported are the observations made by the assessor during these subtests. For example, it is important to know if the student hesitated or took a long time on certain tests that were not under time constraints.

Most subtest scores are reported as scaled scores that have a mean of ten and a SD of three.

Composites

A composite score is when two or more subtest scores are combined. This can also be reported as an index score. Remember, in the case of students with dyslexia, the composite score can be very misleading. The general rule I use when advocating for students with dyslexia is that the use of the composite standard scores alone is not sufficient. If I see an SS of 78 in spelling and an SS of 115 in listening comprehension, I see a problem. So look for those discrepancies in the subtest standard scores. Also, you may see a composite score of 105, which is solidly average, and then look at the subtests and notice that the listening comprehension drove up the composite score— so there is important information in those subtests. Always, always make sure you see all of the standard scores.

The following example is from the Woodcock-Johnson III Normative Update (NU) Tests of Achievement®. This is a commonly used assessment. Subtests on other assessments, such as the Wechsler Individual Achievement Test®-Third Edition (WIAT®-III), are very similar, and the subtest issues are the same.

Table 4.1 WJ-III NU Tests of Achivement® standard scores

Subtest	SS
Broad reading	76
Broad math	124
Broad written language	88
Letter word identification	81
Reading fluency	79
Story recall	121
Understanding directions	109
Calculation	114
Math fluency	114
Spelling	84
Writing fluency	91
Passage comprehension	82
Applied problems	122
Writing samples	101
Story recall-delayed	117
Word attack	99
Spelling of sounds	71

In this example, if you were only offered the broad scores, which are highlighted above, it may look as if this child is doing well in math (which he is) and decently in writing. There is no denying with a score of 76 that this student is struggling in reading. However, when it comes to goals, the subtests in writing tell a different story. The writing samples subtest is bringing the writing score up. A closer look at the spelling subtests of spelling and spelling of sounds reveals a real need for spelling instruction. This would not be obvious if you were just presented with the broad scores, or composite scores, on other assessments. Additionally, based on this child's scores on math we have evidence that he has the ability to perform at a much higher level in both reading and writing. Finally, the high scores in story recall is more evidence that the child understands the information when not presented in print. The subtests tell the true story.

Testing the limits

When an examiner allows a student to take more time on a standardized test or allows them to retake part of the assessment, this is referred to as testing the limits. An assessor will usually divulge that they tested the limits and it is usually noted somewhere in the report. If testing the limits did occur, be sure to find out how it affected the final scores by asking the assessor to explain the observations and make sure it is documented in the report. For a child with dyslexia, offering extra time can make the difference between average and below average on a subtest. However, it is important to know how the child performs under the same conditions as their peers.

Practice effect

A practice effect occurs when a student is assessed more than once with the same or similar instruments. The gains could be attributed to the student's previous experience with the test. Most standardized assessments do not condone testing with the same instrument more than once per year. This is particularly important if you decide to have outside testing (see the section on IEE later) after the school has conducted their testing. Most independent evaluators will want to know what assessments have already been done so that they do not administer the same test and thus possibly invalidate the new findings.

Standardized norm-referenced assessments

Standardized tests are administered under the same conditions for all students. These tests provide information about how your student is performing when compared with their peers.

Criterion-referenced assessments

Criterion-referenced assessments measure how well the student understands specific skills and if they are achieving predetermined objectives. This information is not used to compare the student with his peers. Some examples are: spelling tests, end of chapter tests, and quizzes.

Correct words per minute (CWPM)

When advocating for a student with dyslexia, you will undoubtedly come across the CWPM measure. This is a reading fluency measure that can be used to determine what grade level the student's current reading rate is at. It is important to have a fluency chart with you at the meeting.

But there are some fluency pitfalls to be aware of. First, there is a difference between words per minute (WPM) and CWPM. If you are presented with information that your student is reading at 65 CWPM, you need to ask how many words he read and how many words he read correctly to make sure you understand the complete picture. It is also important to know the conditions under which this measure was collected and if the materials used were created for fluency assessments. Requesting a copy of the passage with the miscues and times noted (when they are non-standardized measures, such as a Read Naturally or Diagnostic Reading Assessment passage) so that you can analyze the miscues will also present very valuable information.

The following is a list of miscues which details the word the student actually pronounced versus what the word actually was. Following the list is an analysis about what the miscues reveal and any observations.

feather for father

her for the

ways for always

coes for comes

listened for laughed

from for farm

very for visit

we're for were

farm for five

house for hens

mother for morning

maid for milk

cows for cow

sheep for showed

then for they

farm for farmer.

These miscues are significant because they illustrate that this child has not mastered the skills necessary to determine how to decode new or unrecognized words. Many of the miscues also indicate that he is guessing based on context or shape, and on many occasions his predictions do not make sense in the passage, thus hindering his ability to understand what he reads.

It is all too common for an IEP team to focus on fluency as a main measure of progress or need. For example, there might be a student with an identified need to improve decoding, spelling, comprehension, and fluency, and the one reading goal that is listed is fluency. While fluency is an important part of the reading process, in order to read fluently, or more fluently, the student needs to work on phonological and orthographic awareness. This is not accomplished by having him work only on fluency. Remember that fluency is the end result of reading and, while it is important, it should not overshadow the need to gather information about all skills related to reading like phonemic awareness, phonological awareness, comprehension, spelling, writing, word attack, and sight word reading.

Informal evaluations

Informal evaluations are often done by general education teachers and resource teachers. They are usually assessments of reading like the Diagnostic Reading Assessment (DRA) and the Qualitative Reading Inventory (QRI). They can also be teacher-made tests, projects, and oral reports. These assessments can contain a wealth of qualitative information that can be analyzed to determine needs. For example, the list of miscues can provide the assessor with information about what the intervention needs to focus on.

Observations

Any school assessment for a child with a specific learning disability (SLD) or suspected SLD is required to include an observation of the student in the general education classroom (Section 300.310 Observation). A short paragraph about the student's behavior and demeanor during the testing does not qualify. In the case of a student with dyslexia, watch for a few things in the observation. Because you are advocating for a student with dyslexia, the observation(s) should be during a time that the student is reading and spelling. This means that an observation during art, PE, music, or recess is not appropriate. The observation should focus on the how the student is performing academically. For example, if it appears that the student was on task and seems to be engaged in the lesson, it seems reasonable that the observer would later check to see what the student actually produced during the observation. It is entirely possible that the student appeared to be engaged and understanding but spelled everything wrong or answered every question wrong. This is vital information.

Below is a useful chart to bring with you to IEP meetings.

Table 4.2 Standardized scores table

Standard score	Scaled score	Percentile rank	Standard score	Scaled score	Percentile rank	Standard score	Scaled score	Percentile rank
145	19	99.9	104	11	61.8	75	5	5
140	18	99.6	103	11	57.9	74	5	4
135	17	99.1	102	10	56.0	73	5	4
130	16	99.7	101	10	52.0	72	5	3
129	16	97.1	100	10	50.0	71	4	3

Standard score	Scaled score	Percentile rank	Standard score	Scaled score	Percentile rank	Standard score	Scaled score	Percentile rank
128	16	96.8	99	10	47	70	4	2
127	15	96.4	98	9	45.0	69	4	2
126	15	95.5	97	9	42.1	68	4	2
125	15	95.0	96	9	39.0	67	3	1
124	15	94.5	95	9	37	66	3	1
123	14	93.9	94	9	34.0	65	3	1
122	14	92.6	93	8	32	64	3	1
121	14	91.9	92	8	30	63	3	1
120	14	91.2	91	8	27	62	3	1
119	14	89.4	90	8	25	61	2	<1
118	14	88.5	89	8	23	60	2	<1
117	13	87.5	88	8	21	59	2	<1
116	13	85.3	87	7	19	58	2	<1
115	13	84.1	86	7	18	57	1	<1
114	13	82.9	85	7	16	56	1	<1
113	12	80.2	84	7	14	55	1	<1
112	12	78.8	83	6	13	54	0	<1
111	12	75.8	82	6	12	53	0	<1
110	12	74.2	81	6	11	52	0	<1
109	12	72.6	80	6	9	51	0	<1
108	12	69.2	79	6	8	50	0	<1
107	11	67.4	78	6	7	49	0	<1
106	11	65.5	77	5	6	48	0	<1
105	11	63.7	76	5	5	47	0	<1

Dyslexia can hide

Dyslexia can hide in the subtests. As the composite scores are an average of all the subtest scores, a particularly high or low subtest score could be overlooked. As these subtest scores can indicate areas of need, it is important to look at each individual subtest score rather than only at the composite scores. So, when you are presented with composite scores that show the student's reading and spelling is in the average or above average range and you know your student is struggling, ask to see the subtests. Remember to ask each assessor which subtests they administered and what they assessed. For example, if a student has average to above average scores in subtests that don't require reading, such as listening comprehension, and those scores are included in a composite reading score, it could inflate the reading score to average, when on further investigation, the subtest scores that have to do with reading skills are below average. Also, some writing subtests only score ideas and not spelling, so check to see what the spelling score is and not just the writing subtest.

Questions you can ask about the testing

Who administered and interpreted the results?

Were any of the tests timed?

Did the student perform worse on timed tasks?

Were any of the tests modified in any way?

Were any subtests not administered? If yes, why?

Why did you choose the particular tests that you did?

If subtests were excluded, why?

It seems that you are dismissing a certain score. Can you please explain why?

Are you relying solely on the discrepancy model to make a determination about eligibility? If so, are you aware that you must also consider other information?

Ask the team to clarify anything you do not understand.

Other assessment data

Once the discussion about the standardized testing scores is finished, it's time to start gathering the other data needed to make a determination about eligibility and areas of need. Here are some suggestions:

- Ask the general education teacher to describe your student's achievement and how that compares to his peers. What are his strengths and weaknesses?

- How is the student doing with spelling? Is he able to retain the spelling of words one or two weeks after the words are taught? Is he able to spell words correctly in unrelated assignments?

- It's okay to ask the team to help you understand what the scores mean. How do they translate to what your student does every day? Ask the team to show you specifically how it relates to your child's classwork and ask to see samples. You want to understand how those scores on those skills affect reading, spelling, etc.

- How is the student doing when he is reading with a time limit?

- Is the student able to adequately answer questions verbally, and how does that compare to his written responses or responses after reading a text?

If your student did not qualify for services and you disagree with the assessment, you can request an IEE at the school's expense. Also, if you have a private assessment or other information that you previously did not share with the team, you can request a new meeting to submit the new information to the team.

GIFTED AND DYSLEXIC: THE TWICE-EXCEPTIONAL STUDENT

Meet Jennifer. Jennifer is in the eighth grade and earning good grades—no, she is getting great grades. According to her teachers she is a nice, compliant, intelligent student who is just a little on the quiet side. Her ideas are complex and interesting and she always wants to do her best.

Jennifer is interesting because her dyslexia is not readily obvious. In fact, the effort it takes her to make all the teachers think she is an average to above average student is probably two to three times that of her peers. Jennifer is a twice-exceptional student, which means she has dyslexia and is intellectually gifted. This means she does three hours of homework when her peers are doing 45 minutes. She writes the same paper three or four times before she lets anyone see it. She chooses smaller words when she is writing to avoid spelling mistakes and receives lower grades because she is unable to showcase her true vocabulary. While we might applaud Jennifer for persevering and becoming successful despite (or because of) her dyslexia, Jennifer would be more successful if afforded the accommodations she needs to level the playing field. Then she could demonstrate what she knows and understands versus what she can write or read in the conventional manner. Her passing of grades and her good performance do not mean that she doesn't need accommodations under the IDEA (Section 300.101 Free appropriate public education), and we need to think outside the box when it comes to how people with dyslexia learn.

Sustained silent reading assessment

On the surface, it looks as if Jennifer's reading and writing are fine and she doesn't need help to access the curriculum, but if we take a deeper look, we will see the struggle. One way to collect data regarding reading fatigue is to have a student read a long passage at their current grade level for four minutes. After each minute, mark where the student is currently reading. After four minutes you should have a word count for each minute. In most cases of students with dyslexia, you will have evidence of fatigue that might look something like this:

Minute 1: 106 CWPM

Minute 2: 96 CWPM

Minute 3: 85 CWPM

Minute 4: 75 CWPM.

Writing with and without assistive technology (AT)

Jennifer will write a sentence like this, "I went on a trip with my mom and dad." This might seem fine until you realize that what she wanted to write was more like this, "Last weekend, my family and I visited the Grand Canyon. It was beautiful with deep canyons and breathtaking views. I enjoyed the time with my family and look forward to our next vacation." How did I know this is what she really wanted to say? I knew because I compared her verbal ability to her written ability.

So, the second way to collect data regarding the writing challenges of a twice exceptional student is to have her write something on her own with no assistance. Then have her dictate something to you and you scribe what she wrote. Lastly, compare the word choice, grammar, and complexity of ideas. Which one is more representative of her true intellect?

Request an IEE

Being denied services or disagreeing with the school's offer of Free Appropriate Public Education (FAPE) is not the end of the road for you. In some cases it is just the beginning. If you disagree with the school's assessment you can request an IEE. You need to submit a request for an IEE in writing, and under the IDEA you are only required to state that you disagree with the testing; however, it is to your advantage to write a detailed request. Here is an example of a request for an IEE at elementary school level:

August 16, 2016

To whom it may concern:

A meeting to determine eligibility for special education services for my student was held at Elementary School in the Elementary School District on Friday, August 16, 2013. Mr. S., the school psychologist who assessed (student) for services, provided the information about his assessment and subsequently determined that (student) was not eligible for services. We respectfully disagree with the outcome and interpretation of the assessment and in accordance with Section 300.502 (a)(1) we are requesting an Independent Educational Evaluation (IEE) at the public school's expense for the following reasons:

1. (student) has documented academic struggles by both elementary school teachers and his family beginning in kindergarten.

2. (student's) phonological processing scores on both the TAPS-3 and the CTOPP were below average (word discrimination subtest and a composite score on phonological awareness of 79 which is in the poor range, according to the CTOPP manual). However, the tester made the determination that the CTOPP score was not truly valid and also mislabeled it low and then threw the score out. Additionally, the examiner determined that (student) did not have a phonological awareness weakness when he averaged subtests from different tests together to get a mean. It is not an accepted practice to

mix subtests from two entirely different assessments to determine a score.

3. The observation did not take into account what the child actually produced during the time he was observed. Because this was a referral for a student who is struggling with reading and writing, what he does during class time in those areas is of the utmost importance.

4. (student) has scores of below basic (bordering on far below basic) on the annual district assessment despite documented average cognitive ability. This is an unexpected weakness that needs to be investigated further.

5. The assessment plan that we signed indicated that the examiner would administer the GORT-4 and that was not done.

6. The CTOPP and the GORT-4 both have new versions (CTOPP-2 and GORT-5) that have been available for over six months and they were not used for this eligibility determination.

7. The examiner made references to (student's) ability to "concentrate" and "focus" despite the observation being devoid of any such behavior or any similar reports by his teachers.

We are requesting an independent evaluation that will include a full investigation into the cause of (student's) documented academic struggles.

We look forward to your prompt reply within a reasonable amount of time.

Sincerely,

Student's parents

There are some things to remember about the IEE (Section 300.502 Independent educational evaluation):

- When a request for an IEE is approved by the school, the school will often provide you with a list of "approved assessors" and ask you to choose from that list. You are not required to choose someone from that list; you can use any professional of your choosing, but they must meet the requirements set forth by the district.

- The district can set a limit of the amount they will be for an IEE. If the person you choose to conduct the IEE charges $2000 and the district only approves $1500, then you are liable for the $500 that is not covered by the district. However, you might be able to have the entire fee paid for if the professional is the only one qualified in your area. If there are excessive travel expenses to get this testing done, those might also be reimbursable.

- Once the IEE is conducted and completed it is sent to the school and added to the student's educational record. This is in contrast to paying for an assessment privately—for those assessments you can choose whether or not you would like to share the private report with the IEP team.

- An IEE that is submitted to the IEP team only has to be "considered" by the IEP team; the recommendations and diagnosis do not have to be accepted by them. However, and this is a big however, if the team does not accept the IEE, they have to explain their reasoning.

- You can only request an IEE once every time a school conducts an assessment.

Here is an example of an IEE request letter at middle school level:

January 3, 2016

Ms. Thomas:

A meeting to determine eligibility for special education services for (student) was held at Middle School in the School District on (insert date). Ms. S, the school psychologist who assessed (student) for services, provided the information about her assessment and subsequently determined that (student) was not eligible for services. We respectfully disagree with the outcome and interpretation of the assessment and are requesting an Independent Educational Evaluation (IEE) at the school's expense for the following reasons:

1. (student) has documented academic struggles by both her elementary school teachers and her family beginning in the first grade.

2. (student's) phonological processing scores on both the TAPS-3 and the CTOPP were below average (phonological segmentation, word memory and number memory forward subtests were all below average on the TAPS-3, and the phonological awareness and phonological memory composite scores were both below average on the CTOPP). Additionally, the CTOPP version that was used is outdated as the CTOPP-2 was released in January 2013, more than a year ago. Lastly, the CTOPP scores were mislabeled as average when they were below average.

3. The San Diego Quick assessment documented that (student's) frustration level for decoding is at the sixth grade level and the IEP team agreed that she was probably at the fourth or fifth grade level for instruction—which is two grades behind.

4. The observation did not take into account what (student) actually produced during the time she was observed. Because this was a referral for a student who is struggling with reading and writing, what she does during class time in those areas is of the utmost importance.

5. (student) has scores of below average on more than half of the tests on the Test of Visual Perceptual Skills (TVPS-3).

6. (student) was referred for reading and writing challenges and the spelling assessment was not given, because she must be assessed.

7. The IEP team made several references to (student's) ability to "concentrate" and "focus" to explain her struggles, despite the observation being devoid of any such behavior or any similar reports by her teachers.

8. According to her report cards, (student's) fluency scores have dropped from basic to below basic from the fifth to sixth grade, indicating that as the content becomes more dense, (student) struggles more to decode. He has also gone from proficient in spelling to basic.

Despite the phonological awareness weaknesses that were in the below average on three different assessments and a visual processing concern in the form of many below average scores in the school assessment, the IEP team suggested that (student) had been taught sufficient strategies by way of guessing the words using context clues. (Student's) documented phonological weaknesses are impacting her ability to read fluently, and the team agreed that fluency was impacted, as is her ability to spell. Therefore, it is necessary to determine the underlying cause of her academic struggles in order to make a fully informed decision regarding her eligibility for special education services.

We are requesting an independent evaluation that will include a full investigation into the cause of (students) documented academic struggles.

We look forward to your prompt reply.

Sincerely,

Student's parents

Interviewing the IEE professional

Choosing the person to conduct the IEE is a very important matter, especially when you suspect the student has dyslexia. Here are some questions to ask the person before you sign on for their services:

- Do you assess for the dyslexia? If so, what is your definition of dyslexia? Do you use the term dyslexia in your report? This is a good time to explain that the term dyslexia is still in the DSM-5 and it is listed under specific learning disorder. Therefore, an assessor is not confined to use only the SLD label; they can be more specific and include the term dyslexia. In fact, the DSM-5 states: "Dyslexia is an alternative term used to refer to a pattern of learning difficulties characterized by problems with accurate or fluent word recognition, poor decoding, and poor spelling abilities." The word dyslexia is in the DSM-5 and it can be used in a diagnostic report.

- Which assessments do you use to determine if dyslexia is present? You will be looking for assessments that assess phonological awareness, phonemic awareness, spelling, reading comprehension, writing skills, math, IQ, and any other areas of concern (e.g. attention, executive function, social emotional needs).

- Are you available to attend an IEP meeting, either in person or by phone or teleconferencing, to explain your report and answer questions? This is not a deal-breaker but rather an added bonus if they can make it. It most cases you will have to pay for their travel and time at the meeting. They might also be available to join the meeting by phone.

- If dyslexia is present, explain how you describe an appropriate intervention. You will be looking for a description of a program, not a brand name, that is based in literacy which includes Orton-Gillingham strategies and/or Structured Word Inquiry (SWI). Some words to be on the lookout for are: multisensory, explicit, phonology, morphology, and etymology.

- What types of accommodations do you recommend for students with dyslexia? See Chapter 9 for a list of appropriate accommodations for students with dyslexia.

- What resources (books, DVDs, videos, websites) do you recommend for parents of children with dyslexia? What resources do you recommend for teachers of children with dyslexia? You will be looking to avoid an assessor who recommends books that are not supported by current research. Chapter 9 has a list of books you can refer to for ideas.

Triennial and early triennial

Once a student qualifies for special education services the district is then responsible for conducting a re-evaluation every three years. This should be a complete evaluation to determine progress and current eligibility. If a situation arises in which you think it would be helpful to determine if progress is being made before the triennial is due, you can request an early triennial. You should make this request in writing with your reasoning. It is important to remember that progress will not always show up on standardized assessments, and you will also need to take into consideration progress in the classroom. A good place to find that progress is from prior IEP meetings where progress on goals was reported and described.

What happens if special education services are denied?

If the IEP team does not qualify your student for special education services, you can do four things. You can accept the decision and consider seeking eligibility under Section 504 (which will be addressed later), where the child would be provided with classroom accommodations. You can also file a state complaint. These are usually simple forms that can be filled out and filed by advocates and/or parents. However, these complaints are usually reserved for procedural violations like timelines and paperwork violations. You can request an IEE. Or you can contact an attorney to determine what the appropriate next steps might be, and please do contact an attorney, not an advocate, regarding this next step. A good advocate will know when it is time to refer to an attorney as they need to be careful that they do not accidentally conduct an Unlawful Practice of Law (UPL).

Unfortunately, a student who is struggling with reading and writing can be denied an IEP for a plethora of reasons, and the district is required to outline their reasons in Prior Written Notice (PWN). This may leave you feeling helpless, upset, confused, and angry. You know your student is struggling. You know there is a problem, but the team did not find a problem that was "big" enough for them to offer special education services. Below are some reasons a child with dyslexia may be determined not to be eligible for services, and suggestions for how you might respond. Remember, if your student is found not eligible it may be time to contact an attorney. This book does not cover due process or mediation because those are processes that are best explained by special education attorneys. I have listed a short explanation of next steps that you might take with an attorney:

> *Resolution session*—When due process is filed, the district is required to schedule a resolution session. This is done to try to resolve the dispute before it goes any further.

> *Mediation (formal)*—Mediation is a confidential meeting that is held prior to due process. Like resolution, this meeting is intended to get the parties to come to an agreement before the case goes to a hearing.

> *Due process*—Due process is an administrative hearing that, usually, is attended by your attorney, and the case is decided by a judge (administrative hearing officer).

Denied eligibility scenarios

IEP team: *The student did not meet the discrepancy (or severe discrepancy) requirement to receive services.*

While a school can use this method as part of the way to determine eligibility, they can also use other means to aid in the determination of eligibility, such as teacher reports, parent reports, report cards, state testing, outside tutor reports, and school samples (Section 300.306 c (1)(i) Determination of eligibility). If you believe that "other means" were not considered, you can bring that to the team's attention and ask that they explain why that other information did not impact their decision.

IEP team: *The student isn't two grades behind.*

This is the waiting-to-fail model and it is not supported in the IDEA. Nowhere in the IDEA is there language stating that a child has to be two grades behind to qualify for service. In fact, all you have to do is meet the two-pronged approach to eligibility. First, do they have a disability? Second, is that disability affecting their academic performance? Then the team determines if the child requires special education services to be successful in the general education classroom. If the team sticks to the "two grades behind" rationale, or something similar, you can ask for the district's written policy. In this case, you would be asking the district to supply you with the policy that states a child has to be two grade levels behind to be eligible for services. It is hoped that this will be a learning experience for the entire IEP team, as they will learn that that policy does not exist.

IEP team: *There isn't an obvious need for reading, but the team dismisses the identified need for spelling and writing.*

The SLD category includes "written expression" in its definition (Section 300.309 (a) (1) (iii) Determining the existence of a specific learning disability). So, when you hear that they don't qualify students who only need help with writing, this is a prime opportunity to provide the team with the definition of SLD and highlight the written expression. Spelling is as much a need as reading. I will cover much more about the important of orthographic awareness in the next chapter.

IEP team: *Well, Tom is at high school now and we don't really teach reading in high (or middle) school, so we can only offer a study skills course.*

The bottom line is that if a student qualifies for special education services and they have an identified need in the area of basic reading and spelling skills, those needs require specialized academic instruction. If a school says they don't offer what the child needs at their school, then contact an attorney immediately. Services cannot be denied when the needs are identified. Schools can also pay for reading services outside the school system if they refuse to offer them. Study skills classes are not direct instruction in basic skills. If your student is in middle school or high school and the IEP team is not responding to his individual needs, it might be time to consult an attorney.

In these scenarios, you should always ask the school to show you the law that supports this reason for denial of services.

The eligibility process can be very frustrating, and if your child does not qualify, you might find yourself asking if it is worth the hassle, money, and emotional toll it can take. The answer is entirely up to you and what is best for your situation. Just remember that whichever path you take it is the right path because it's your path and no one knows your child better than you. If you decide to move forward, then the next chapter will help you develop an effective IEP.

CHAPTER 5

What does a good IEP look like?

First things first, what is an IEP?

An IEP is an Individualized Education Program (IEP) and it is a legal document. It outlines the student's present levels, goals and services (Section 300.320 Definition of Individualized Education Program). These will each be explored in detail in this chapter.

Before we even get started on what should be included in a good IEP, we need to be clear about who writes the IEP, who has input, and who can make changes to it. The answer to all of the above is the entire team, and the team includes the student's parent and/or guardian and anyone with knowledge about the student. A pre-written IEP that is handed to you as a draft or suggested IEP is acceptable, if submitted as preparation and not a final copy, but an IEP that is handed to you as final and complete with little to no participation by you is not acceptable, and in some cases could be deemed predetermination, and predetermination is not okay. The team cannot predetermine placement without input from the team (which includes the parent) about alternative placements and/or interventions. When this does happen it can be construed as a denial to allow the parents to participate in a meaningful way.

The IEP document

There is not a standard IEP format and they vary widely from district to district, but there is a similar sequence for IEP documents and they usually go something like this:

- Background information

- Eligibility category(s)

- Parent concerns

- Present levels

- Goals

- Accommodations

- Services

- Special factors

- Notes (whether or not this is included varies widely).

So you can see that IEPs follow the *needs drive goals and goals drive services* model. We will go through them one by one. But before we do that, you might want to brush up on some common things said at an IEP meeting so you will be ready with the cold, hard facts.

What you may hear during the IEP writing process

During the IEP writing process you may hear absurd things about dyslexia and reading. Here are a few you should prepare for and how you can respond:

Dyslexia is not real—It is still hard to believe that people still believe this, but they do. Here is a tip: gather as many resources as you can about dyslexia, from reputable sources—there are many listed in Chapter 9—and present this information to the team who is making this claim. It is important that you do this *on the record* so that you have a date that the team "knew or should have known" about the student's dyslexia. It can also be effective to bring all the materials and books you have about dyslexia and plop them down on the table as you sit down. You may never refer to them or look at them, but they are there and that is often enough.

Dyslexia is a broad term—I love this one. It's almost as if no one has really taken the time to really think about what they are saying. This is usually followed up with, "Dyslexia is part of SLD so it is very broad." The fact of the matter is that SLD is the broad or "umbrella" term, as several qualifying conditions are listed under SLD, including dyslexia. You can remind the team with the resources you gathered for the "Dyslexia is not real" comment and educate them about the very specific symptoms of dyslexia.

We don't work with kids with dyslexia—Yes they do and they always have, no matter what they called it. You can remind the team that dyslexia has been included in the IDEA since 1974. You can refer them to the October 15, 2015 Dyslexia Guidance memo.

Spelling isn't important—I think I have covered this one pretty sufficiently in this book, but the short answer is, of course it is, and written language is covered under specific learning disability (SLD).

Her cognitive scores show she will probably have difficulty reaching these goals—Wait, what? Low expectations are not acceptable. A student who qualifies should be able to begin to close the achievement gap, and the school needs to provide whatever services are required to help that happen.

We don't need all these goals—This is simple, if there are ten needs, there are ten goals. Period.

We just use a bunch of different things with a student in special education—This is also know as the "eclectic approach" and it is not appropriate. A student who has an IEP requires an individualized plan that responds to their individual needs. The eclectic approach was also not accepted by Congress when they clarified that any approach needs to be individualized and research-based and is inappropriate for a student with dyslexia.

Now that you are ready to educate the team about dyslexia, it is time to complete the IEP.

Background information

This is the easy part of the IEP meeting. This is where the basics are included like name, address, phone, email, parents' names, date of entry into special education, next triennial, gender, and ethnicity. Easy peasy. You've got this.

Eligibility category

To be eligible for special education services, a student must qualify under at least one of 13 eligibility categories. They are:

- autism

- deaf-blindness

- deafness

- emotional disturbance

- hearing impairment

- intellectual disability

- multiple disabilities

- orthopedic impairment

- other health impairment

- specific learning disability

- speech or language impairment

- traumatic brain injury

- visual impairment (including blindness).

In this book, we are addressing the needs of children with dyslexia, or suspected dyslexia, so the eligibility category should be listed as specific learning disability (SLD). Remember that dyslexia is listed as a qualifying condition under the umbrella term of SLD. In many cases there will be a secondary category for a student with dyslexia which is usually other health impairment (OHI) or speech and language impairment (SLI). This part of the IEP is not usually an issue, but an appropriate category should be correctly identified. However, it can become an issue when there are three eligibility categories and there is only room for two to be listed. You need to determine a primary disability and then decide which one to leave off. This does not mean that the student will not receive services for that disability; it simply means that the form is not adequate. This should be documented somewhere else in the IEP document.

Parent concerns

This is your opportunity to voice your concerns as you see them at home and from your perspective. Be as specific as you can and as lengthy as you want to be. If you think your child has dyslexia, include that in this section. It is a great way to document that you have expressed ongoing concerns. Also, be sure to update this section from IEP to IEP, which could be year to year or more frequently if you have supplemental IEP meetings. It can be very powerful for a parent/guardian to read a pre-written impact statement at the beginning of the IEP writing process. This statement should describe how dyslexia has impacted on the student and the family. It is not a time to point fingers or place blame, just to describe and submit for the student's educational record. This will help the team remember that the IEP should be individualized and that there is a student at the receiving end of it. Below is an impact statement to give you an idea of what it might look like (you might want to have some tissues nearby):

EXAMPLE OF AN IMPACT STATEMENT

Two-and-a-half years ago my ten-year-old daughter Frances, aka Frannie, was diagnosed with dyslexia. That diagnosis not only changed her life and how she understands herself, but it changed our entire family's life too. Now I know it's not a death sentence, and it's not the end of the world either, but it has brought unexpected challenges in raising my daughter that I simply did not expect. For instance, I thought she would go to school and learn to read. When that didn't happen, I was really scared. At the time, I didn't know what dyslexia was and neither did her teachers. She was super intelligent and artistic, but her difficulties with words and even sounding out letters was baffling. It was when first and second grade came around and decoding words became a must, that I said, "Something is wrong."

The private school Frannie was going to did not understand or provide help with her challenges. In an attempt to acquire better resources, she transferred to a public school in mid-second grade, where she qualified for an IEP, which was to be implemented at the beginning of third grade. As third grade began, her peers were again passing her up and it was evident that the bus had left the depot, and she was still there. Tears and stomach aches were commonplace. Her self-esteem was crushed, and trying to keep up in class literally made her nauseous and dizzy. Absences were abundant, as were illnesses, and she was anxious and disturbed at this point. She was struggling to read at a first grade reading level, and math has always been excruciatingly difficult as well. As a mother, it is devastating to see your child suffer...and not learn. The helplessness and devastation that I felt compelled me to start researching learning disabilities and reading disabilities. This is when I discovered a local dyslexia center, where they proceeded to diagnose, remediate, tutor, and advocate for my severely dyslexic daughter.

The diagnosis was a profound turning point for Frannie. It solved the mystery and validated every experience and challenge she had had up to that point. It was an utter relief to her (and to me and her dad) to know that there was a name for this, an explanation that made sense, and most of all there was help. She started private tutoring immediately.

I was hopeful that with a comprehensive IEP at school and specialized tutoring through the dyslexia center, third grade would get better, but it didn't. A parents' open house with her third grade teacher revealed that Frannie was not just being sensitive and dramatic about her school experience. When I asked her teacher how she was doing he proceeded to tell me that she was not doing well, that she couldn't keep up and the class was way over her head, that she was so worried and anxious that he was afraid she would get an ulcer at eight years old, that as a parent I should be really worried, and that there was probably a better school for her somewhere else. She never went to his class again.

Frannie would come home from school with stacks of incomplete work that she and I would work on together. Dyslexic students need processing time to think and when she received this time and explicit help at home or with the dyslexia center, she was open to learning and not anxious. We got somewhere. Therefore, when it became more productive to work with her at home and it was actually counter-productive to her learning and well-being to go to school, I decided to homeschool her. I quit my corporate accounting job and have dedicated my life to helping this little girl learn how to read and get through school with as little blunt force trauma as possible.

We spent the rest of third grade homeschooling, tutoring, and helping her work on her self-esteem again. In fourth grade her confidence made a great recovery because she was ready to return to class twice a week. We are fortunate to be a part of a charter homeschool where kids can go to school twice a week, and learn at home three days a week. It keeps them socially active and involved. An appropriate IEP has been established for her and she is receiving several hours of special education services a week. However, critical years were lost in Frannie's education because early intervention and remediation did not take place, therefore the likelihood of her ever getting out of special education is rare.

Since we now know dyslexia is inherited, Frannie's diagnosis answered a lot of questions for my husband, Robert, as well, such as his own lifelong challenge with reading fluently and his struggles in school. When he was nine he remembers a woman (I'm presuming a psychologist) coming to his house to help his parents figure out "what was wrong with him." This psychologist proceeded to test Little Bobby by having him crawl on the ground on all fours, and declared that he didn't crawl enough as a baby, which had impeded his ability to learn and distinguish right from left. Evidently he had to do a series of eye movement exercises as well, but the worst part for him was the look on his parents' faces. He now identifies with that anguish his parents felt for their child.

We have come so far with scientific research and evidence over the last 15–20 years, explaining what dyslexia is, how it manifests itself in the brain, and how these children can be identified (early) and remediated properly so they don't end up in special education for their entire school careers. My thoughts have shifted from "something is wrong with my child" to "something is wrong with the educational system." Even today this information has not reached the classroom. I have yet to meet a teacher who understands and has been trained in dyslexia. I have been told by school teachers and administrators that they do not recognize, diagnose or treat dyslexia and that it is a medical issue, not an educational issue, in addition to a plethora of other ludicrous statements. This lack of knowledge and help being passed down through the generations is astounding. These students deserve to learn and their instructors deserve to have the tools necessary to teach. Why this isn't happening is beyond me...and my child, so we will continue do our best to educate them.

Present levels of performance and of academic achievement and functional performance—"Just the facts please"

This is where you need to start paying close attention to what is written. The purpose of this section is to help you describe your student's current academic abilities in a manner that is quantifiable. It should be clear enough for anyone to read and gain a pretty good understanding of your student's *current* achievement in reading and writing. This is not the place for personal judgements or subjective opinions; this is the place for scores from standardized and informal assessments. Let's take a look at an example for Teddy, who is in third grade.

TEDDY'S PRESENT LEVELS

Current present level for reading: Teddy is reading near grade level. He is currently completing work samples at a mid-third grade level. He continues to segment words when decoding, and uses visual cues to help with comprehension.

What it should look like: Teddy is reading at late second grade text with 98 percent accuracy (independent level) as evidenced by Accelerated Reading (AR) texts and the Woodcock-Johnson® (you should replace this with the measurements that are available at your school). He is currently reading third grade texts with 50 percent accuracy, which is still at frustration level, as measured by the Analytical Reading Inventory (ARI). Teddy currently reads 72 WPM, which is equivalent to the second grade level. Teddy currently has difficulty decoding multisyllabic third grade words, which is affecting his fluency. Teddy relies on picture cues to aid comprehension. He needs to continue to receive specialized academic instruction to meet his individual reading needs.

Current present levels for written language: Teddy has made progress in spelling. He still spells phonetically, but his accuracy has improved slightly. Teddy also writes stories in a logical order.

What it should look like: Teddy continues to spell phonetically with little regard to syllable types and spelling rules. According to the Test of Word Spelling (TWS-5) he currently spells at first grade level. Teddy also struggles to spell first grade level sight words. When given support, Teddy can write a logical story.

Current present levels for math: Teddy is doing well in math. He is currently at grade level with calculation skills.

What it should look like: Teddy is able to perform addition, multiplication, and division at third grade level with 98 percent accuracy. Teddy does have difficulty word problems.

You are part of the team, so you are able to contribute your suggestions to making this part of the IEP as accurate as possible. Remember that as the child progresses through school you are looking for progress, and looking to close that achievement gap; the present levels will help you determine if progress is being made. Finally, be sure that this is updated every year. It is not uncommon to see present levels remain the same for three years because the IEP team is under the mistaken impression that they only change when a triennial is completed—this is not how it works.

Goals

BASELINE DATA

Every goal has to be preceded with baseline data. This is data that measuring specific skill at the beginning of the current IEP. If the goal is reading fluency, then the baseline will describe the current CWPM of the student along with the grade level. Without this information it is difficult to determine if progress was made or how much progress was made. The baseline data should be just that, data, not observation or subjective or vague comments. Anyone who reads the IEP should be able to determine the student's current skill level based on the baselines and present levels.

Unacceptable baseline example—Student has difficulty reading words with more than one syllable or student reads dysfluently.

Acceptable baseline example—Student can decode 20 of 50 polysyllabic words that contain vowel teams and diphthongs.

PROGRESS ON GOALS

Once an IEP is in place, the IEP team reports the student's progress on goals before creating the next IEP. This is an extremely important part of the process and you need to keep track of the data. If a goal is not met, then the team needs to explore why that goal has not been met. If there has been progress toward the goal and everyone is satisfied with that progress, then you can include the same goal on the new IEP, but with new baselines and higher standards. Remember that the goal of an IEP is to close the achievement gap, so keeping the goal exactly the same is not going to do that.

Now, if a goal is not met, it is not okay just to dump the goal and move on to something else. If the goal was an identified need and is an important part of the student's literacy, instead of erasing the goal and moving on, the team needs to find out what it is about the current services that are making it difficult for the goal to be met. Many times, this is a red flag that the services offered are not appropriate.

Here is a chart to help.

Table 5.1 Documentation of the goal, and progress

	Goal 2012	Goal 2013
	Jason will read a third grade passage at 90 CWPM	Not included in new IEP
Goal met? Evidence?	N/A—Initial IEP	Goal not met. According to present levels he is reading a fourth grade passage at 63 CWPM. Middle of fourth grade should be reading 112 CWPM (50th percentile)
Baseline	WJ-III—SS 89 (not a measurable baseline)	Teacher record of 63 CWPM using a fourth grade text
Present need? Where is it identified?	Yes. Teacher records indicate Jason is having difficulty in this component of reading	Yes. Identified in present levels of 2012 and 2013 IEP

GOALS, GOALS, GOALS

Goals are the heart of the IEP document. These are the skills that your student should be learning during the academic year and they are far too important to gloss over. They need to be poured over. They need to be derived from the needs, which is the information in the "Present levels" section. They need to be individualized, which means they are not restricted to goals that are pre-written in a drop-down menu. I was tempted to include an entire chapter with template goals, but that would defeat the individualization that is required, so instead let's look at what an unacceptable goal looks like and how to create good, measurable, individual goals.

Parents have asked me how important the goals really are. Remember: needs drive goals and goals drive services. The school is responsible for the goals that are set and agreed on in the IEP. If they are low or incorrect and the IEP is signed, the school is responsible for these goals. The goals need to be written so that the child receives educational benefit and the goals can be accomplished with appropriate instructional approaches. For example, if there is a need for fluency improvement then there should be a goal for that. If there is a need for better spelling, there should be a goal for that. If there is a need for sight word improvement, then there should be a goal for that. If there are ten needs, then there are ten goals. There is no limit to the number of goals an IEP can have. Let's take a look at a few goal-related scenarios.

GOAL WRITING SCENARIOS
Scenario one

IEP team: *We did not include a fluency goal because he is only reading 12 words per minute correctly right now, so what is the point in teaching fluency?*

When I heard this I have to admit, I was speechless while I gathered my thoughts to respond. When fluency is a need, the IEP should include a fluency goal. Fluency is the ultimate goal of reading and needs to be taught and practiced from day one. Make sure the baseline has a present CWPM (correct words per minute), not just a grade level. The goal CWPM should be high enough that it would be noticeable and measurable progress and starting to close that gap. Additionally, the fluency tool to assess should be the same for progress monitoring. The progress monitoring tool should be designed for progress monitoring and not a random reading passage.

A word about CWPMs

It is very important to ask the following questions when interpreting fluency measurements.

- Was this a cold read or a hot read? A cold read means the student has never seen the passage before. This includes even a quick run-through before reading. If the student read the passage six months earlier, it is still not a cold read. If it is not a cold read, then request that a cold read be done and that score reported. The purpose of a fluency goal is to help the student read unfamiliar text independently.

- CWPM and WPM are different measures. You will want to know what is being reported, the number of words they read correctly in a specified amount of time or the number of words that are in the passage? Don't forget to ask for evidence from which they derived this information to make sure it was intended to be used as a fluency measure.

Scenario two

IEP team: *We did not include a phonological awareness goal because we have a vocabulary goal.*

This is simply a lack of awareness of the reading process. If a child is struggling with single-word reading, non-word reading, spelling, and/or fluency, then it is a need and they require a phonological awareness goal. Vocabulary and phonological awareness are not one and the same; in fact they are two entirely separate components of reading. Phonological awareness teaches the student to understand and manipulate the language by understanding that graphemes represent phonemes, syllable types, and spelling rules. This is accomplished using a multisensory, structured, explicit, and sequential program. Because we are talking about students with dyslexia, they will almost always need a phonological processing goal.

A note about methodology

It is imperative that the program being used is documented somewhere in the IEP—usually in the Notes section. Many IEP teams will state that they do not include the names of programs in the IEP document because if the student changes schools and the next school does not have that program, it will be problematic. However, you can remind the team that Congress clarified the importance of methodology, and stated that the child's IEP should include "a statement of special education, related services and supplementary aids and services, based on peer reviewed research." The Department of Education clarified that IEPs must include "research-based methodology," and it was also stated whether or not methodology can be included in an IEP, "if an IEP Team determines that specific instructional methods are necessary for the child to receive FAPE, the instructional methods may be addressed in the IEP."

Scenario three

IEP team: *We don't really teach spelling, we just do worksheets and weekly tests. With technology these days students don't really need to know how to spell anyway.*

For students with dyslexia, this is disastrous. The fact of the matter is that most teachers and curriculum developers do not know how to teach spelling. The IDEA includes written expression as an area of disability, and if a child cannot spell, then they have to be taught this skill. It should not be up to the IEP team to determine who learns to spell and who doesn't. The purpose of teaching spelling is not to create perfect spellers, but to teach the student, especially the student with dyslexia, how English is organized. Section 300.8(c)(10) states, if...the child does not achieve adequately for the child's age or to meet State-approved grade-level standards in one or more of the following areas, when provided with learning experiences and instruction appropriate for the child's age or State-approved grade-level standards: (i) Oral expression. (ii) Listening comprehension. (iii) Written expression. (iv) Basic reading skill. (v) Reading fluency skills. (vi) Reading comprehension. (vii) Mathematics calculation. (viii) Mathematics problem solving.

Think about this. If a child can read a word, it does not mean they can spell it, but if a child can spell a word, they can certainly read it. This is because the student understands the morphological boundaries of a word and how that affects its pronunciation. Additionally, a child who understands how to spell a word based on its morphophonemic structure will become a better reader. The bottom line is that it is not okay to withhold the right to learn to spell because it is viewed as something that can be "fixed" with spellcheck. If there is a need to improve spelling, then there is a goal for spelling. Additionally, this should be a stand-alone goal, not grouped in with sight words or a writing goal that includes spelling under editing. Editing is not explicit spelling instruction.

Here is an example of an acceptable, measurable spelling goal with high expectations:

New goal: *When presented with a list of 50 multisyllabic third grade words that includes closed, open, and vowel–consonant–e syllable types, John will spell them with 90 percent accuracy.*

GOAL WRITING

To write a good goal, you should familiarize yourself with the SMART goal, which is an acronym that is attributed to Peter Drucker's management by objectives concept. Peter Wright of Wrightslaw changed the A to make it more relevant for IEPs. I added an additional R for reasonable. The acronym stands for:

- Specific

- Measurable

- Use action words

- Realistic and relevant

- Reasonable

- Time bound.

So, when writing goals, the following questions need to be answered:

1. It there a specific skill being targeted in this goal or are there multiple skills that need to be broken down? In the case of dyslexia, is the need for spelling embedded in an editing goal? If so, it should probably be made into its own goal so it can be measured separately.

2. Is this goal measurable? Is there a clear way to determine if progress is being made?

3. Are there action words in this written goal? How is the goal going to be achieved? How will it be measured?

4. It is realistic? This can be an interesting discussion. Some members of the team might be inclined to set the bar low so that the goal can be met and say that it is realistic. However, we have to keep in mind that we need to close that achievement gap, so the bar should be raised, and if the services need to be increased to meet the goal, then that is what should happen. However, you do want to remember the other R that I added to this acronym, which is reasonable.

5. Are you being reasonable? We all want these bright children to succeed, but we also don't want to set them up for failure. Set the bar high but don't demand a goal that is unreasonable. For example, if a fifth grade student is reading at second grade level, it is unreasonable to create a goal that she will be reading on grade level in one year.

6. Is it time bound? This is fairly easy because IEPs are, by nature, time bound. Every goal has a year to be met and in some districts there are benchmarks throughout the year.

Real proposed goal: *John will be able decode multisyllabic words that include words with long vowel sounds (a, e, i) in words like* **turmoil** *and* **chipper**.

Did you find the problems? Are you stunned? Embarrassed for the author of this goal? It is very common to see goals like this and this is a fabulous illustration of the importance of nit-picking the goals. Here are the problems:

1. Where are *o* and *u*?

2. What grade level? How many words?—Where is the measurable part of the goal?

3. The goal states that only one concept will be learned in a year (the long vowel sound of only three of the vowels).

4. Last, but certainly not least, *turmoil* and *chipper* do not contain long vowel sounds!

Below is the same goal rewritten.

New goal: *When given a list of 50 fourth grade polysyllabic words John will be able to accurately decode polysyllabic words which will contain closed, open, vowel teams, and vowel-consonant-e (beside, statement, remain) syllable types with 90 percent accuracy as measured by teacher records.*

This new goal includes more than one syllable type, which means John is expected to learn more than the original goal suggested, it is measurable, and, most importantly, the words used as examples are correct and show an understanding of what he will actually be learning.

BENCHMARKS AND TEACHER RECORDS

Not all districts require benchmarks on an IEP, but for those that do, make sure that progress is expected at each benchmark. Usually benchmarks correspond with reporting periods. Also make sure that the benchmarks are written in a way that makes pedagogical sense. For example, closed syllables should be mastered before open syllables in an Orton-Gillingham approach.

It is very common to be reviewing progress on goals and to ask for the teacher-kept data in order to review what was done over the year to make progress on goals and be told that the teacher did not keep records. So, when creating goals, be very specific how that teacher-kept data will be collected, and how often it will be collected.

GOALS ARE NEEDY

Sometimes goals are just glossed over, or even worse, totally ignored and just shared as an after thought during the IEP meeting. But goals are the window into what the IEP team understands about the identified and individual needs of your student. They highlight what the goal writer, who is often the person providing the instruction, knows about the reading and spelling process. The goals are what your student is going to learn over the course of an entire year; they deserve your attention. And just like services, goals have needs too.

Goals have needs too

Need #1: They need to make sense. If you have to read it more than two times to try to figure out what it means, it needs help.

Need #2: They need to have high expectations for progress (but be reasonable). The purpose of the IDEA is to close the achievement gap. It is not unreasonable to expect at least a year's progress in a year's time, but to close the gap, we often need more progress. However, four years' progress is not reasonable.

Need #3: They need to be pedagogically sound. The person teaching the student is supposed to understand how to teach reading and spelling. If they do not have a solid foundation in how to teach a student with dyslexia or the reading process itself, it will be evident in the goals.

Need #4: They need to respond directly to identified needs. If the student has six needs in the areas of reading and spelling, they have six goals, period. While some of the areas of need can be taught simultaneously, they need to be measured separately. (And yes, spelling is a need.)

Need #5: They need to be understood by anyone who reads them. It is always a possibility that the teacher will change or the student will move during the course of an IEP. Can anyone who picks up the IEP understand the terminology in the goal?

Need #6: They need to be individualized. While drop-down and template goals are convenient, they are not individualized. Goals should be a direct result of the individual student and their academic needs. If template goals are used, they must be modified to fit the student. Also, if a template goal or drop-down goal does not exist for the need, then create the goal. There is nothing preventing the writing of original goals.

Need #7: They need to be reviewed often. Benchmarks (if used) should be monitored. If progress is not being made on goals throughout the year, then the services and goals need to be re-evaluated.

Need #8: They need to be a team effort. Pre-written goals are a starting point; consider them a suggestion.

Need #9: They need to be SMARRT, specific, measurable, achievable, realistic, reasonable, and time-bound.

Let's take a look at another proposed goal. For reference I read this goal at least eight times to try to figure it out and then sent it to a colleague to see if had lost my mind:

When given letter patterns containing consonant blends, and letter patterns containing long and short vowel patterns and irregular vowel patterns (i.e. r-controlled) in random order, Daniel will orally combine these elements to create recognizable words with 75% accuracy in two consecutive trials as measured by teacher observations.

Need #1: It doesn't make sense.

Need #2: It has low expectations with 75% accuracy and two trials. Additionally, only learning long and short vowels is not enough for third grade.

Need #3: The terminology in this goal bears no resemblance to any reading and spelling progression. It is almost nonsensical.

Need #4: It does respond to a need, so we can check this one off.

Need #5: I think it's safe to say no one understands this goal.

Need #6: This is definitely not from a drop-down menu.

Need #7: This was not included in this goal. Not all districts require benchmarks.

Need #8: According to the parents, this was not a team effort.

Need #9: This goal is far from SMARRT.

So, what can we do with a goal like this? How about this:

When given a list of 40 third grade polysyllabic words that contain closed, open, vowel-consonant-e and r-controlled syllables, Daniel will accurately read the list with 85% accuracy in three consecutive trials as measured by curriculum-based assessments.

There we go, I think that the goal is satisfied and less needy. Let's do one more goal that left me perplexed:

Given grade level instruction and multiple opportunities, he will be able to identify multisyllabic words in a grade level text with 80%

accuracy, as evidenced by his ability to read whole grade level fluency probes, by the end of the IEP term.

Need #1: It doesn't make sense. What is "whole grade fluency" anyway? What does "identify" mean? Is he actually going to read the word or point it out?

Need #2: There is no way to determine expectations as grade levels and type of reading level is not indicated.

Need #3: The terminology is appropriate when read individually, but together it doesn't make pedagogical sense.

Need #4: It appears to respond to a need, but is it a fluency need or a decoding need? Remember that we don't know what "identify words" in this goal actually means.

Need #5: I think it's safe to say no one understands this goal.

Need #6: This is definitely not from a drop-down menu.

Need #7: This was not included in this goal. Not all districts require benchmarks.

Need #8: According to the parents, this was not a team effort.

Need #9: This goal is far from SMARRT.

Let's help this goal assuming that the need for this seventh grade student is to read polysyllabic words:

When given a list of 50 seventh grade polysyllabic words that contain free and bound bases as well as affixes, Daniel will accurately identify the morphemes and then read the list with 85% accuracy in three consecutive trials as measured by curriculum-based assessments.

So, be sure to give the goals the attention they deserve. They are begging to be fussed over.

OVERVIEW OF GOALS: COMMON NEEDS, RATIONALE AND TEMPLATES

As I stated before, goals are the heart of the IEP and unfortunately there is little or no training on how to write a good goal. Before you begin, remember that there is no limit to the number of goals in an IEP. If there are ten documented and agreed-on needs, then there are ten goals. Reading is a complex task that encompasses at least five different components and each one should be measured separately. As stated earlier, spelling should not be embedded in an editing or writing goal. Students with dyslexia need to be explicitly taught to spell. Asking a student with dyslexia to go back and find their misspellings for editing or to look for the correct spelling in a passage or dictionary is not explicitly teaching them the underlying structure of English, which is what research shows is the most effective and appropriate way to teach these children.

Okay, now for the practical stuff. Below you will find information about making your case for common areas of need for students with dyslexia and the goal templates. Please use them as a template only and adjust them to meet the individual needs of your student.

DEFEND YOUR GOALS

In order to advocate for good goals, you have to be able to articulate why those goals are appropriate for a student with dyslexia. Below are some basic reading and spelling skills that you will likely advocate for, and some advice about how to articulate what they really mean and how to describe these skills to a student with dyslexia.

COMMON AREAS OF NEED

Phonemic awareness

Phonemic awareness is the ability of the student to be able to manipulate the language before graphemes are introduced. So this is strictly about being able to hear a word or part of a word and verbally identify the individual phonemes. For example, ask the student how many phonemes there are in the word <cat>. The correct answer is /c/ /a/ /t/. If the student is having difficulty with this task, they may answer something like /c/ /at/ or they may not understand the task at all. This is an indication that they are not hearing the individual phonemes in the word or don't understand the concept of the separation of individual phonemes. A goal for phonemic awareness will be appropriate for a student who performed below average on assessments that assess this skill. Some examples are the CTOPP-2 and the TAPS-3 (not including the cohesion index). Not every student with dyslexia will need to work on this skill.

What is a phoneme?

The Blackwell Encyclopedia of Writing Systems defines a phoneme as, "a group of similar speech sounds signified by an alphabetic letter." For example, if a child spells the word <try> as <triy> they have identified that there are four phones in the word <try> but only three phonemes. It is important for professionals who are interpreting assessments, and creating and implementing education programs, to understand these types of errors in order to respond effectively.

Phonological awareness

Phonological awareness is the ability of the student to pronounce and manipulate graphemes (letters) and the phonemes they represent. This applies to the ability to read and spell words. For example, a blending exercise consists of using manipulatives that have graphemes in them, and the student is given phonemes and tasked to identify the graphemes that represent those phonemes to create a word. The student is then taught to blend the graphemes in order to pronounce (read) the word. This can be done with full words or parts of words. A student with dyslexia often has difficulty with phonological awareness. The severity of the difficulty with this reading and spelling skill varies widely and the goal should be written to address the current level of difficulty. Again, not all students with dyslexia will show a deficit in phonological awareness.

Orthographic awareness

Orthographic difficulties occur when someone has average or above average phonemic and phonological awareness, but they have difficulty translating that ability to the written word. It is imperative to analyze a student's writing sample; in fact it is the first thing I look at and it usually reveals everything I need to know about what the child understands about the written language. When a child who is struggling with dyslexia scores well on the phonemic awareness and phonological awareness assessments but is struggling with spelling assessments, they need to improve their orthographic awareness.

MEET JAVIER

Javier performed at the average to above average range on phonemic and phonological awareness tasks. In fact, he scored in the above average range in phonological awareness and phonological memory on the CTOPP-2, but he still struggled to read, and was only able to spell words that had a perfect sound to symbol relationship. For example, he was able to spell words like *brandish*, but not the word *who*. So, could it still be dyslexia if his phonological skills were intact? Yes, yes, yes!

This type of academic difficulty is what I am classifying as orthographic dyslexia, which is why students like Javier need to improve their orthographic awareness. Now, I may use the term a little differently from others. According to the *Oxford Dictionary*, orthography is the conventional spelling system of a language.

Understanding English orthography requires that students understand how words are structured, which does need a basis in phonology, but if the student is unable to translate their adequate phonological awareness skills to the written word, then it stands to reason that they have an orthographic processing deficit, and the intervention should focus on how the written language is structured. This is orthographic dyslexia. Dyslexia can occur when a student fails to make the transition from the phonological stage to the orthographic stage.

Schwa and language stress awareness

Students with dyslexia often struggle to spell words like <every> and <different>, spelling them <evry> and <difrent>. If this is the case with your student, then they need to develop schwa and stress awareness. This will be a new concept at most IEP meetings, but it is very important for a student with dyslexia to understand how to find the stress in a word in order to understand why the unstressed vowels of a word are not fully pronounced, and sometimes not pronounced at all, which is called schwa deletion. A schwa and language stress awareness goal will help a student understand that <every> contains the second <e> because the base word is <ever> and the suffix is <y>. Now she can see that when we pronounce the word <every> we delete the second <e> which is a schwa, but will understand the reason that <e> has to be represented in the spelling of the word. As with all of the skills a student with dyslexia will be working on, teaching this concept explicitly will be the key to their success. One way to determine if this is a need is to analyze a writing sample from the student and determine if the words she misspelled included a schwa. If a significant amount misspelled due to the schwa, then it is a need.

Are you schwaducated? Take this quiz to find out

It is not uncommon to sweep the schwa under the rug or give it a cursory nod in a short lesson and then move on. Instead, many instructors choose to over-pronounce a word and avoid the schwa altogether. Think about this— the schwa is the most common utterance in the English language and it deserves to be understood. Here is a quiz for you to become schwaducated, and when you are done you can peruse the answers to learn more about the schwa.

1. English written language is based on syllables.
   T   F

2. The words <every> and <different> have schwa deletions.
   T   F

3. The schwa occurs in the unstressed part(s) of a word.
   T   F

4. The word <the> contains a schwa.
   T   F

5. The word <every> contains a schwa.
   T   F

6. Which part of the word <fantastic> is stressed?

   a. fan

   b. tas

   c. tic

7. A student can hum a word to find the stressed part of the word.
   T   F

8. The schwa is too complicated to teach to younger students.

      T   F

9. A word may or may not have a schwa depending on the accent of the speaker.

      T   F

10. How many schwas are in the word <problem>?

    a. one

    b. two

    c. none

Answers:

1. False. English is a stress-timed language, not a syllable-timed language. This is why there seem to be so many "exceptions" when teaching with syllables. See the link to *Rachel's English* in the References section, under "Websites".

2. True. Check out number 6 (and then read the rest of the article) in the *Lexicon Valley* article in the References section (under "Websites").

3. True. Now that you have watched the video about stress-timed languages you can now begin to learn how to find the stressed part of a word. Hint: number 7 of this quiz has a helpful tip.

4. True. The word <the> is often taught as an exception, but the fact is that <the> is usually unstressed in a sentenced, which explains the spelling. If you emphasize <the> by saying, "That was *the* best ice cream I have ever had," the <e> is pronounced.

5. True, but it is a deleted schwa. See number 3.

6. b. A good tip we learned from Gina Cooke (see the References section, under "Websites") was to call the word to dinner or get the word in trouble in order to find the stressed part of the word.

7. True. Try it with the word <tenacious>.

8. One hundred percent false! It is essential for anyone learning to read and spell English as their native language or a second (or third or fourth) language to understand the reason for discrepancy between our spoken words and our spelling. It should not be skipped or given a cursory tip of the hat, but studied and understood. Think about this—just about every polysyllabic word contains a schwa. Here are some examples: impossible, elevator, watermelon, convertible, calculator, harmonica, kindergarten, information, celebration.

9. True. Accent plays a very big role in whether or not a schwa will be present. For example, I met a French woman who pronounced each syllable in the word <Florida> where many Americans delete or schwa the <i>.

10. a. However, if you have heard a Canadian pronounce the word <problem> you might not hear a schwa at all.

So, let's hear it for the schwa and go and continue your schwaducation. It's vitally important to understand our language, and our children, especially those with dyslexia, deserve to get *all* of the information, not just what we think they can handle.

Morphological awareness

Morphological awareness is the student's ability to identify the meaningful parts of a word. Now, when this is brought up at an IEP meeting, you will inevitably hear, "Oh yes, we already do that, but we reserve that for older students." Herein lies the problem. Morphological awareness should begin on day one of kindergarten, especially for children with dyslexia. A goal for morphology should include making sure the student understands what a base is and how to locate the affixes. The student should also be able to verbalize what the affix does to the grammatical purpose of the word. For example, give the student the word <play> and have them add <-ed>, <-ing> and <-s>, then ask the student how and if the word meaning and purpose change with the different suffixes. Then try it with prefixes.

Sight words

Sight word and high-frequency words are used interchangeably and that should not happen in your IEP meeting. High-frequency words are often decodable and included in sight word lists because students should be able to recognize them instantaneously, but this is different from a sight word. Some examples of high-frequency words are: the, if, will, that. An IEP for a student with dyslexia should focus on the sight words that don't readily appear to be decodable by sounding them out. Some examples are: sign, two, debt, doubt, know. When using a structured literacy approach, like Orton-Gillingham, a student with dyslexia will learn to memorize these words using various techniques such as the sight word study method. Improving this skill will improve their fluency and comprehension and, in many cases, their spelling.

When using a linguistics-based approach, such as Structured Word Inquiry (SWI), the goal would be to investigate and find out why each letter is a word. For example, the teacher can show the student that when they add the suffix <-al> to the word <sign> the <g> is pronounced. There is a list of resources regarding this approach in Chapter 9.

Reading comprehension

It should be fairly obvious why a student would need a reading comprehension goal, but there is one thing to watch out for when advocating for students with dyslexia. It is common to have a student with dyslexia struggle through a passage and still be able to comprehend what they read. In this case, comprehension is not a need, so it does not need to be a goal. Now, you want to make sure they comprehend fiction as well as non-fiction, so make sure to investigate those nuances in the scores and teacher reports. It is also important to note if a student can adequately decode and comprehend, and if they do so slowly. If this is the case, it might be a situation where accommodations versus an IEP might be appropriate. Students with dyslexia are likely to struggle with fluency even after remediation, and that is okay. It's better to be correct than fast.

Fluency

As stated above students with dyslexia almost always struggle with fluency, which is a combination of reading rate, prosody, and comprehension and is usually measured by CWPM. However, many parents are presented with IEPs that are using a fluency goal as the only goal to teach reading, and this is unacceptable. By now you know that if a student has ten reading and spelling needs, then they have ten goals; fluency is only one of those needs. A common program used for fluency is Read Naturally, and while it is an appropriate intervention for fluency, it should not be used for any of the other reading and/or spelling goals. This goes for any other fluency programs that are offered as an "intervention." When advocating for a fluency goal, make sure you study the section where I explained the difference between CWPM and WPM and cold and hot (or warm) reads. Additionally, make sure that this goal is not receiving the most amount of direct service time—that time should be spent on the other components of reading and spelling that study the structure of the language.

Vocabulary

Like reading comprehension, the need to strengthen vocabulary should be fairly easy to explain, but make sure that it is truly a need. Also like reading comprehension, some students with dyslexia have a very sophisticated vocabulary and don't need to use specialized academic instruction (SAI) time to work on this skill.

Writing

Students with dyslexia often struggle with writing, not because they do not have the thoughts and ideas necessary to create thoughtful and profound responses to academic questions, but because they are often hindered by spelling, and when that spelling is requiring an inordinate amount of cognitive energy, there is little left over to think about syntax, grammar, and organization. For example, a student with dyslexia is likely to use the word <big> instead of <enormous> because they cannot spell <enormous> even though it is in their verbal vocabulary. So the need for this goal should respond to the individual writing needs of the student.

NOW THAT YOU KNOW HOW TO EXPLAIN THE NEEDS, LET'S WRITE THE GOALS

Now that you have explained the need for the goals for a student with dyslexia, it is time to write the goals. Remember that goals are supposed to be reasonably calculated so that the student will make more than trivial progress. Additionally, the purpose of the IDEA is to close the achievement gap, so a goal that suggests a student will make a year or more of progress in one academic year is not unreasonable. The fact of the matter is that if that type of progress did not happen, then the gap would never close. Goals are supposed to be individualized, so if the team states that they don't have a goal for what you are suggesting or it is not in their drop-down menu, you can politely remind them that goals are supposed to respond to individual needs, so let's go ahead and create some goals.

Phonemic awareness goal template

By (insert one year from the date of the IEP) the student will be able to add, delete, and manipulate individual phonemes in one-syllable words and one-syllable words with affixes that are presented verbally with 90 percent accuracy, as measured by teacher-kept data.

Phonological awareness goal template

By (insert one year from the date of the IEP) the student will be able to decode a list of (insert number) previously unseen one- and two-syllable words which shall include closed (cat, belt, blast, intact), open (me, open), and vowel-consonant-e (decide, take) words that are presented in isolation with 90 percent accuracy, as measured by teacher-kept data.

By (insert one year from the date of the IEP) the student will be able to decode a list of (insert number) previously unseen one- and two-syllable words which shall include vowel team (tea, seam, teem), diphthongs (boy, toil, town, brawn), r-controlled (cart, shirt, hurt), and consonant-le (able, bubble, sparkle) words that are presented in isolation with 90 percent accuracy, as measured by teacher-kept data.

By (insert one year from the date of the IEP) the student will be able to decode a list of (insert number) previously unseen polysyllabic words, which shall include all of the syllable types (fantastic, holiday), which are presented in isolation with 90 percent accuracy, as measured by teacher-kept data.

It is a good idea to provide example words in phonological awareness and spelling goals so that anyone who reads the goals will understand the terminology. Remember that IEPs should be written so that anyone can understand them.

Schwa and language stress awareness goal template

A common misconception is that English is a syllable-timed language and it is actually a stress-timed language. What this means is that students, especially students with dyslexia, need to be explicitly taught the role of the schwa in English and how it affects our reading and spelling. For example, in the word <method>, the <od> in an unaccented syllable and is pronounced as /əd/, but when the student discovers, the word <methodical>, they understand why the <o> is in the word.

To help improve the student's ability to read and spell words that contain a schwa, a goal can be written the following way:

By (enter date one year from this IEP) when given a list of 25 words containing a schwa in the beginning, medial, and/or final position of a word, the student will be able to identify which grapheme is representing the schwa phoneme and explain how that is affecting the pronunciation and spelling of the word with 90 percent accuracy, as measured by teacher-kept data.

Morphological awareness goal template

By (enter date one year from this IEP) when given a list of 25 words containing a free base and prefixes and affixes (playing, mistrust, unedited) the student will be able to successfully identify the free base, the affix, and the grammatical use of the affix with 90 percent accuracy, as measured by teacher-kept data.

By (enter date one year from this IEP) when given a list of 25 words containing a bound base and prefixes and affixes (detached) the student will be able to successfully identify the free base, the affix, and the grammatical use of the affix with 90 percent accuracy, as measured by teacher-kept data.

When proposing these goals do not allow yourself to be talked into the "we do morphology later" argument. For a child with dyslexia, this is part of the explicit instruction of the English language they require to improve reading and spelling.

Sight words goal template

By (enter date one year from this IEP) when given a list of 50 previously unseen (insert grade level) sight words (not decodable) the student will successfully decode the list with 90 percent accuracy, as measured by teacher-kept data.

By (enter date one year from this IEP) when given a list of 50 previously unseen (insert grade level) sight words (not decodable) the student will successfully encode the list with 90 percent accuracy, and as measured by teacher-kept data.

Reading comprehension goal template

By (enter date one year from this IEP) when the student reads a (enter grade level) non-fiction text they will be able to identify the main idea of a text and explain how it is supported by key details, and summarize the text.

By (enter date one year from this IEP) when the student reads a (enter grade level) fiction text they will be able to compare and contrast the point of view from which different stories are narrated, including the difference between first- and third-person narrations.

Fluency

For fluency goals, you will need to have an expected fluency by grade level chart with you.

By (enter date one year from this IEP) the student will be able to read a (insert grade level) previously unseen and unstudied text with (enter number based on grade level fluency chart) CWPM, as measured by teacher-kept data.

Because the CWPM is the number of words read correctly, there is no need for the extra percentage. For example, a common way to write this goal is:

By (enter date one year from this IEP) the student will be able to read a third grade passage that is previously unseen and unstudied text at 85 CWPM with 85 percent accuracy, as measured by teacher-kept data.

Here the 85 percent accuracy would actually bring the CWPM down to 72 CWPM.

Spelling (Orthographic Awareness) goal template
This goal is usually the encoding version of morphological awareness.

By (enter date one year from this IEP) when given a list of 25 words containing a free base and prefixes and affixes (playing, mistrust, unedited) the student will be able to successfully encode (spell) the free base, the affix, and the grammatical use of the affix with 90 percent accuracy, as measured by teacher-kept data.

By (enter date one year from this IEP) when given a list of 25 words containing a bound base and prefixes and affixes (detached) the student will be able to successfully encode (spell) the free base, the affix, and the grammatical use of the affix with 90 percent accuracy, as measured by teacher-kept data.

Writing goal template
By (enter date one year from this IEP) the student will be able to write opinion pieces on topics or texts, supporting a point of view with

reasons in three out of four drafts, as measured by teacher-kept data and student samples.

Accommodations

If you ask a successful adult with dyslexia, like Ben Foss, author of *The Dyslexia Empowerment Plan*, how they made it through school, they will almost always tell you they did it with the love and support of their loved ones and accommodations. Those accommodations were both high and low tech. If a child is eligible for an IEP, they are eligible for accommodations, and this includes assistive technology (AT).

It is important for the IEP team and the student to understand that accommodations are in place if the student chooses to use them. For example, if the accommodation states that the student should not be required to read out loud, but she raises her hand, then she should be called on to read. Here are accommodations that are helpful for students with dyslexia that can be included in the IEP. Remember that accommodations should be individualized, so not every accommodation will be appropriate for every student.

Reading

- Provide access to audiobooks

- Provide access to text-to-speech software

- Provide a set of textbooks for home use

- Only ask the student to read aloud if they volunteer

- Provide extra time for reading assignments

- Allow the student to preview reading materials.

Spelling

- Reduce spelling lists

- Do not take off points for spelling errors on written work

- Allow access to a spellcheck

- Provide access to word prediction software.

Writing

- Provide a scribe

- Provide access to speech-to-text software

- Offer alternative projects instead of written reports

- Provide written copies of notes

- Minimize the amount of copying from the board

- Allow the student to use a keyboard to take notes

- Allow the student to record lectures

- Reduce written work

- Provide graphic organizers

- Grade assignments on content rather than form.

Homework

- Reduce homework

- Allow the student to dictate answers

- Allow typewritten homework

- Limit time spent on homework

- Email list of assignments to the student or parent.

Testing

- Allow the student to take tests orally

- Provide for extra time

- Read directions aloud

- Read test questions aloud

- Provide alternatives to testing (oral projects or videos)

- Provide a quiet testing area with minimal distractions

- Grade in collaboration with a special educator

- Clarify or simplify written directions.

Don't forget that you can and should request AT from the school district. The IDEA defines AT as "any item, piece of equipment, or product system, whether acquired commercially off the shelf, modified, or customized, that is used to increase, maintain, or improve functional capabilities of a child with a disability" (Section 300.6(a) Assistive technology service). The IDEA also requires "IEP Teams to consider the assistive technology needs of all children with disabilities." The school cannot use the lack of funding or lack of availability of any device as a reason to deny AT for a student with dyslexia.

Finally, the IDEA defines AT as "any service that directly assists a child with a disability in the selection, acquisition, or use of an assistive technology device. (A) the evaluation... (B) purchasing, leasing, or otherwise providing for the acquisition of assistive technology devices... (C) selecting, designing, fitting, customizing, adapting, applying, maintaining, repairing, or replacing... (D) coordinating and using other therapies, interventions, or services with assistive technology devices... (E) training or technical assistance for such child, or...the family of such child (F) training or technical assistance for professionals."

Services—offer of FAPE

Finally, you've hashed through the IEP document, and this is where the rubber meets the road. Once again, we are back to the needs drive goals and goals drive services mantra. This is the point of the IEP meeting when you find out just what the school is going to provide by way of direct services to help your student meet their goals. This will look remarkably different from district to district, but the general principle is the same—are the services appropriate to meet the needs and goals of the individual child? Here are some questions to ask regarding services:

- Who will be providing the instruction?

- What program will they be using? (Yes, they have to tell you.) See the earlier note about methodology.

- How many students will be in the group with my student?

- Do the other students have similar needs as my student?

- How often will I receive progress reports?

- Will a paraprofessional be working with my student? If so, what are their qualifications?

- When can I send someone in to observe?

FAPE SCENARIO

Natalie is a fifth grade student who is currently reading at second grade level. She has difficulty decoding multisyllabic words, she struggles with spelling, her fluency is slow and halting, and she tends to write very short sentences. She has four goals for each area of need and is offered 30 minutes of push-in services per day.

Natalie is three years behind in reading and spelling and she has the documented need to improve basic reading skills, which show a need for direct instruction in a pull-out model. A push-in service means that Natalie will have a teacher (or a paraprofessional) in her classroom. This usually means that someone is there to help her with the work that is taking place in the classroom; however, this means she is not receiving the direct service she needs. This is not an acceptable situation. It is your right to bring such a concern to the IEP team and begin a conversation about how Natalie can receive services that are appropriate.

In Natalie's case she is three grade levels behind, and in order to close that gap she needs direct, explicit instruction that takes place in a small group or a one-to-one basis. If she is in a small group it should be a homogeneous group of no more than three students taught by someone who is trained in multisensory, explicit, systematic research-based instructions. You might ask, how will the proposed services help Natalie meet her goals and close the achievement gap? What will the services look like? Is the proposed program research-based?

MIDDLE AND HIGH SCHOOL SERVICES

Advocating for a student who struggles with reading and writing in middle and high school is very difficult and it is difficult for several reasons. The main reason is because teachers in middle and high school are content area teachers and most are not trained in reading instruction, so they do not have the training necessary to understand the needs of these children. This is not an assault on teachers; it is a statement of what they are trained to do, and teaching children to decode and spell and is not part of that training. Having said all of that, middle and high schools are still responsible for providing the services that a child needs, even if it is basic decoding and spelling. I wish I had a dime for every time I heard this in a middle or high school IEP meeting, "We don't teach reading or spelling at this level." Really? So, this child just doesn't get the opportunity to learn to read and spell? We are back to the needs of the child driving the services; spelling is a need, therefore it is a service that must be offered and delivered. You can also write a follow-up letter and submit it to the team to be attached to the IEP document.

Special factors

In general this section does not affect a student with dyslexia (unless they have other comorbid conditions). However, this is where the use of AT will be checked, so make sure that if the student has qualified for AT that this is checked. It is not enough for the school to say that they already provide technology; this needs to be documented as it might become very important when the student requests accommodations in high school and college.

Notes

There is usually someone assigned to take notes in an IEP meeting and these notes are very important. Make sure that at the end of the meeting, the notes are read back to the IEP team, and don't hesitate to request to add anything that you think should have been included or anything that needs correcting. In an ideal world, you are recording the meeting, so you can go back and listen to what went on to determine if the notes are correct. In the case that you not recording, you will want to take your own notes during the meeting, which you can submit to the team to be added to the IEP document and become part of the student's educational record. The notes can be the place to document a diagnosis of dyslexia. It can also be the place where the methodology is listed.

HOW TO NAVIGATE COMMON DIFFICULT SCENARIOS

Scenario One

The team agrees to a certain methodology but refuses to document it in the IEP because they say that if you move, then that holds the new school accountable to implement the same program. What you can do is remind them that you are part of the IEP team and would like to document what you agreed to during the meeting. Remember to ask for the district's written policy about methodology if you need to.

Scenario two

The team has proposed to offer your student an eclectic approach— you know, a little of this and a little of that. Remind the team that a student with dyslexia needs an individualized approach and that you, as the parent/advocate, want to participate in the process of choosing the appropriate methodology.

Scenario three

During the meeting the parents disagree with the methodology that is being proposed and there is a lengthy discussion around this topic. When the notes are read back, this conversation has not been documented. The parents request that this conversation be captured in the notes and the team agree. Again, remember, you are part of the team, so don't hesitate to ask these questions.

Related services

The IDEA (Section 300.34 Related services) defines a related service as:

a) Related services means transportation and such developmental, corrective, and other supportive services as are required to assist a child with a disability to benefit from special education, and includes speech-language pathology and audiology services, interpreting services, psychological services, physical and occupational therapy, recreation, including therapeutic recreation, early identification and assessment of disabilities in children, counseling services, including rehabilitation counseling, orientation and mobility services, and medical services for diagnostic or evaluation purposes. Related services also include school health services and school nurse services, social work services in schools, and parent counseling and training.

In the case of dyslexia, related services are usually services like speech therapy and occupational therapy that can be offered separately from SAI time or on a consultation basis. A consultation basis means the occupational therapist or the speech and language pathologist (SLP) will consult with the teachers who are working with the student to help them help the student meet any of the SLP or OT goals. Consultation is really the bare minimum of services, and in most cases it is preferable to find out why they are offering consultation instead of direct services. When related services are offered as a direct service they add hours to the student's time out of class, so that is something to be considered. You should ask yourself if the related service is worth the extra time outside class. For example, OT will not help a student learn to spell, but it might help with other symptoms of dysgraphia. So, if the student is being offered OT for spelling, then you might want to ask the occupational therapist how their service will improve the spelling.

It is common to assume that SLPs solely work with articulation problems and disorders, but they also work with communication skills. So, if a student scores poorly on the cohesion index of the TAPS-3 assessment and there is concern about their ability to communicate effectively, then speech and language therapy might be an appropriate related service.

To sign or not to sign

The end of the meeting is near, the water bottles are half empty, the cookies are gone and everyone is wary, then they push the signature page your way and ask you to sign the completed IEP. What do you do? In most states (remember to check your state regulations), you have the right to sign for attendance only, and I recommend this in most cases, even if you like the IEP. Give yourself permission to sleep on it and read it through, think about it, and then if you are still satisfied, sign it. If you are not satisfied and you disagree with it, then don't sign it. A little-known tidbit is that you can sign and approve parts of the IEP and not others. So, if you are satisfied with the math goals and proposed services, then by all means, sign for the math services only. Any pressure to sign documents at a meeting is unwarranted. But remember that services will not begin until you sign the IEP. If there was a previous IEP in place, that IEP remains active until the new IEP is signed; this is referred to as a "stay put."

Remember...

Read the IEP from the top down. The present levels need to include data, not observations. Goals should be directly derived from assessments and progress monitoring and they should be SMARRT. Every need should be addressed. Goals drive services, so if the goals are incomplete, low, or inaccurate, the services will be incomplete and ineffective. It never hurts to ask an expert to read the IEP and get a second opinion. For students with dyslexia, goals can be very tricky, but they are the pinnacle of the IEP—make them count.

You disagree with parts of the IEP. What can you do?

When it appears that you have reached an impasse with the IEP team or there are parts of the IEP that you just don't agree with, it can be a good idea to adjourn the meeting without signing the IEP, or sign for attendance only, and write a letter explaining your disagreement. This letter then becomes part of the student's educational record.

CHAPTER 6

After the IEP: Keep Your Eye on the Ball

The IEP meeting is over, there was hand-shaking, niceties were exchanged (or not), documents were signed, and the work has really only just begun. Once an IEP is signed the services can begin immediately. But remember to be reasonable—if the school needs a week to set up the schedule, give them the week. In this chapter I will share a few things you can do to make sure the intervention is being implemented with fidelity, and that there is consistency in the services.

You can request an observation

In the world of advocacy and dyslexia, observation seems to be a seriously underutilized tool. In fact, observation can be the one thing that can turn a situation around and create some positive change, but it has to be done correctly. The observer needs to know what to look for and what to report. It may also come as a surprise, but one of the most heart-wrenching things I do as an advocate and dyslexia expert is classroom observation. There have been observations where I have actually felt nauseous the longer I've sat and watched the instruction. The reason for my visceral response is usually the "instruction" the student I am advocating for is receiving, but it is also caused by the students in the class for whom I am not an advocate—who is watching out for them? I take solace in the thought that advocating for one student will have a ripple effect for others. So, what could provoke such a response to what should be an innocuous experience? Below I have described why an observation should take place and what the observer should be evaluating. I have also shared some very common experiences that occur in classrooms with students with dyslexia.

WHEN AND WHY SHOULD A CLASSROOM OBSERVATION TAKE PLACE?

A classroom observation should take place in the following situations:

- The student is not making progress, but the school is not willing to issue an IEP.

- The student has an IEP and is not making progress.

- The student has an IEP and the intervention needs to be evaluated.

- The student is receiving services from an aid instead of a fully credentialed teacher.

- The school has changed the intervention or the teacher.

- In preparation for an upcoming IEP, due process, or mediation.

WHO SHOULD CONDUCT THE CLASSROOM OBSERVATION?

- The observer should be someone the student does not know. If the student knows the observer it is likely to create a less than authentic observation.

- The observer should have an understanding of dyslexia. This person should be looking to see if the intervention is being implemented with fidelity.

- The observer should know how to take notes and how to write a detailed report that can be submitted in an IEP meeting and during legal proceedings.

WHAT SHOULD THE OBSERVER BE LOOKING FOR?

Time management and pace: The observer should note what time the instruction actually began and when it ended. There should be notes about the student's effort during instructional time. Many times there will be comments by teachers that the student is off task or disengaged during instructional time and that is what is contributing to their lack of progress. The observer has the opportunity to determine if and when this happens. I observed a child who had been described as extremely distractible and with a bit of a classroom behavior problem. What I observed was a student who was in a group that moved far too quickly, with little to no explicit instruction. What they described as distractible, I observed as a coping mechanism for frustration and the feeling of a lack of power to change it. This observation comes in handy when negotiating for a more appropriate placement.

Report example: *The lesson moved at a very rapid pace and there was no explicit instruction. The lesson consisted of the teacher reading the directions from a workbook and giving answers. In 30 minutes, the group covered four different reading components without any explanation of the concepts being taught.*

Teaching strategies: Many schools are defending the curriculum they choose by stating it is structured, systematic, phonics based, and centered on the National Reading Panel (NRP) results—but this is only half the battle. The teaching techniques employed by the teacher are equally important, and the observer can determine if the teacher is teaching using multisensory techniques, explicitness, and questioning strategies, and including repetition and review. One of the most common and troubling observations I have made is that teachers are not using questioning techniques to direct students to the correct answer or to help them develop independent thinking and reading skills. Additionally, students are told to read things, repeat things and spell things, but they are never asked to explain how they can correct a word they misspelled or a word they read incorrectly. They are not given the tools to use to help them determine how to decode independently. And last but certainly not least, what does the teacher do when the student makes a mistake or gets stuck on a word? Does the teacher give the answer to stop and teach the answer? The answer to this question is of the utmost importance.

Report example: *The group then moved into a spelling activity. The teacher dictated words and the students spelled them. She did check to see if they spelled them correctly but she did not do any teaching to help them figure out why it was misspelled. She then dictated a sentence which had a word that was difficult for them to understand because of the teacher's accent, and she did repeat it for them several times. When they were done, she wrote the sentence on the board and asked the students to correct their sentences. She never asked them to read their sentences or talk about the types of errors they made. The student appeared to do his best and was on task the entire portion of the lesson. There was no explicit teaching about spelling rules and or asking questions about their mistakes.*

Program being used: Most IEP teams will not specify programs to be used but may give some examples. So, during the observation it is imperative to find out which program is being used, what chapter the student is currently working in and if any other programs are used when the observer is not there. Write down the title and author so you can check to see if it is research-based, multisensory and age-appropriate. For example, I observed Zachary using a program that was written for fourth to sixth grades and students who need "some extra help." Many districts use a program because the author has a good reputation in the reading community. The problem is that Zachary is in the first month of the third grade and needs much more than "some extra help."

Report example: Student was using Phonics for Reading and was on Lesson 11.

Expertise of the teacher: During an IEP it is important to ask the teacher what their experience is in the area of dyslexia and teaching those with diagnosed dyslexia. In many cases, the teacher or the district rep will respond that they have a mild/moderate or similar credential in special education. However, under No Child Left Behind (NCLB) legislation, anyone working with a child with reading disabilities is required to be highly qualified in the area of reading. So, if you can't get a straight answer about the qualifications, the observation is the next best thing. The one red flag I always notice is a teacher's over-reliance on the workbook instructions and almost no ability or confidence to improvise to make sure the student understands. A highly qualified reading teacher will know when to slow down, repeat, question, and explain. A teacher simply following a curriculum will move too fast, give answers instead of questions, have children echo read instead of independently read, and is not able to adequately teach spelling.

Report example: Very quickly, the group moved into oral reading. The student read out loud and struggled significantly with the passage. When he came to a word he had difficulty decoding (i.e. the word whale) the teacher gave him the answer. She said, "No, it is /w/ and the end is /t/." She gave him the answer several times and at no time did she teach him decoding strategies so that he could decode the words independently. She repeatedly said "ah-ah" indicating the answer was wrong, but never guided him to the correct answer.

Collect any work that was produced during the observation: Something that has always been perplexing to me is the type of observation done by the school psychologist. It does not seem to differ based on the child's disability—and it should. They will describe the classroom, the student's behavior, and the assignment and then write a summary. My question is always, "Did you look to see what they actually did while you were observing?" They always look at me as if I have two heads. This is an observation of a student with dyslexia—someone who is struggling with reading and writing—so if they appear to be "on task" and "appropriate" during class, then you need to see what they are producing during that on-task behavior.

Report example: *Once the observation was complete I took note of what Zachary had written during the writing portion of his lesson. He wrote the following sentence (sic): The Wale (whale) wuz gry. Although Zachary was on task during this lesson, he was still unable to complete the task and I did not see any instruction to help him with his spelling.*

A few things to remember

- Before any observation can take place, the school has to be notified and they will determine a good time for the observation.

- Because the school will be aware of the observation, it cannot be expected that the observation will be a 100 percent authentic representation of what happens on a daily basis. I like to think it is the best they can do, so if it is inadequate the day they know you are coming, then you can make the assumption it is not as good the days you are not there.

- Take notes, but try not to be intrusive. Don't ask questions during the observation—be a fly on the wall.

You can request an IEP meeting as needed, but be reasonable

If you are concerned about a lack of progress, the intervention being used, or have any other concerns during the year you can request, an IEP meeting. You do not have to wait until the annual IEP to convene a meeting. Once you request the meeting, the school has 30 days to schedule and hold this meeting. Remember the extra R for reasonable in the SMARRT goal section of Chapter 5; you should also remember to be reasonable when requesting additional IEP meetings. Requesting a meeting for every little issue will not benefit your student. You can communicate with the team via email and phone calls for less pressing matters. But you should absolutely call a meeting if a student is not making progress.

Progress reports

Remember the purpose of an IEP is to help the student close the achievement gap. In most districts you will receive progress on goals every time report cards are issued. However, you can ask for more frequent progress reports. But remember that a child with dyslexia will usually not make measurable progress in a short amount of time, so quarterly reports are a reasonable expectation.

Beginning of the year meetings

At the beginning of each year it is a good idea to request an IEP meeting (remember that the school has 30 days[1] to hold that IEP meeting) to discuss the IEP and accommodations. Since it is more than likely there will be new general education teachers, it is a prime opportunity to bring information about dyslexia as well as a brief description of your student, a copy of your impact statement, and a little information about the student's accommodations.

No one will care about your student like you do. Staying on top of an IEP or 504 plan is a part-time job that should be taken seriously. Don't be afraid to ask questions about progress and programming, but also allow the teachers the opportunity to implement what you agreed to; be reasonable but vigilant. A school year can and does go by quickly—what happens during that year is of great importance and should not be taken lightly.

1   Always remember to check your state laws about timelines.

CHAPTER 7

Section 504

When a student does not qualify for an IEP or you decide that accommodations would be sufficient, you might consider a 504 instead. What is a 504? Section 504 of the Rehabilitation Act is a federal law that requires a school district, which receives federal funds, to provide Free Appropriate Public Education (FAPE) to each child with a disability in the district. Section 504 states that: "No otherwise qualified individual with a disability in the United States…shall, solely by reason of her or his disability, be excluded from the participation in, be denied the benefits of, or be subjected to discrimination under any program or activity receiving Federal financial assistance." The Office of Civil Rights (OCR) states that Section 504 requires districts to provide to students with disabilities appropriate educational services designed to meet the individual needs of such students to the same extent as the needs of students without disabilities are met. An appropriate education for a student with a disability under the Section 504 regulations could consist of education in regular classrooms, education in regular classes with supplementary services, and/or special education and related services.

Reasons for a 504 over an IEP

There are a few different situations in which a 504 is put into place instead of an IEP:

- The student did not qualify for an IEP but still demonstrates a need for accommodations to access the general education curriculum due to a documented learning disability. For example, Mathew did not qualify for an IEP but he still finds reading large quantities of material very difficult due to his dyslexia and it takes him twice the amount of time to read the same material than his peers. When he is allowed more time to read or is given less material to read, he is able to perform at his expected level.

- The student is receiving services outside the classroom and only needs accommodations in the general education classroom. Madeline does qualify for an IEP but her parents have opted to have her receive services outside of the district instead of through the school. However, she still needs accommodations while in the classroom.

- The student has received intervention and is now transitioning to an accommodations-only model. Cynthia is in the seventh grade and she has had an IEP since the second grade. She is now reading at grade level but still struggles with writing. She would like to transition to using assistive technology to help with her writing.

How to initiate a 504 plan

Like an IEP, a 504 plan can be initiated by the parents/guardians or the school. Also like the IEP process, If the school initiates the 504 process and the parents/guardians do not agree to the 504, the school can proceed without consent. However, in order to do so, the school has to file for Due Process. For complaints and support about the 504 process, parents/guardians should contact the Office for Civil Rights (OCR).

Eligibility

A child is eligible for a 504 plan if they have a disability and that disability is affecting their ability to learn in a general education classroom. This includes learning disabilities and is described in Section 504 the following way:

> Major life activities, as defined in the Section 504 regulations at 34 C.F.R. 104.3(j)(2)(ii), include functions such as caring for one's self, performing manual tasks, walking, seeing, hearing, speaking, breathing, learning, and working. This list is not exhaustive. Other functions can be major life activities for purposes of Section 504. In the Amendments Act (see FAQ 1), Congress provided additional examples of general activities that are major life activities, including eating, sleeping, standing, lifting, bending, reading, concentrating, thinking, and communicating.

Much like the assessment process for an IEP, a district is also required to assess for 504 eligibility. This process is described in detail in 34 C.F.R. 104.35(b) the following way:

104.35 Evaluation and placement

(a) Preplacement evaluation. A recipient that operates a public elementary or secondary education program or activity shall conduct an evaluation in accordance with the requirements of paragraph (b) of this section of any person who, because of handicap, needs or is believed to need special education or related services before taking any action with respect to the initial placement of the person in regular or special education and any subsequent significant change in placement.

(b) Evaluation procedures. A recipient to which this subpart applies shall establish standards and procedures for the evaluation and placement of persons who, because of handicap, need or are believed to need special education or related services which ensure that:

(1) Tests and other evaluation materials have been validated for the specific purpose for which they are used and are administered by trained personnel in conformance with the instructions provided by their producer;

(2) Tests and other evaluation materials include those tailored to assess specific areas of educational need and not merely those which are designed to provide a single general intelligence quotient; and

(3) Tests are selected and administered so as best to ensure that, when a test is administered to a student with impaired sensory, manual, or speaking skills, the test results accurately reflect the student's aptitude or achievement level or whatever other factor the test purports to measure, rather than reflecting the student's impaired sensory, manual, or speaking skills (except where those skills are the factors that the test purports to measure).

(c) Placement procedures. In interpreting evaluation data and in making placement decisions, a recipient shall (1) draw upon information from a variety of sources, including aptitude and achievement tests, teacher recommendations, physical condition, social or cultural background, and adaptive behavior, (2) establish procedures to ensure that information obtained from all such sources is documented and carefully considered, (3) ensure that the placement decision is made by a group of persons, including persons knowledgeable about the child, the meaning of the evaluation data, and the placement options, and (4) ensure that the placement decision is made in conformity with 104.34.

(d) Reevaluation. A recipient to which this section applies shall establish procedures, in accordance with paragraph (b) of this section, for periodic reevaluation of students who have been provided special education and related services. A reevaluation procedure consistent with the Education for the Handicapped Act is one means of meeting this requirement.

What to know about a 504 plan

There can be some confusion about the difference between a 504 plan and an IEP. Here is a chart to help you understand the differences.

Table 7.1 Differences between an IEP an a 504 plan

	IEP	504
Provides direct services	Yes	Usually not
Provides accommodations	Yes	Yes
Requires goals	Yes	No
Has timelines	Yes	No
Is required to be a written document	Yes	No
Requires parent consent	Yes	Not specifically required
Requires procedural safeguards	Yes	No
Requires reevaluation	Yes—every three years	Yes—before significant change of placement

	IEP	504
Dispute resolution	Office of Administrative Hearing—resolution/mediation/due process	Office of Civil Rights (OCR)

A 504 plan can be a good option, but it often needs to be revisited and parents bear the responsibility of making sure it is being followed. It is not uncommon to find out that accommodations are not being provided pursuant to a 504 plan, so you will need to make sure your student is able to self-advocate for those accommodations. It can be helpful to write a new teacher a short note about the accommodations in the 504 plan and why they are necessary.

I also think it is very important to note that accommodations are there for the student if she needs them. If the student makes the decision that they do not want to use an accommodation at a particular time, then that is perfectly okay. For example, an accommodation for a student with dyslexia might be that they are not required to read in front of their peers. But if your student raises her hand and wants to read, then they should be allowed the opportunity—this is the true nature of accommodations.

College-bound students

The transition to college can be overwhelming for most young people, but students with dyslexia need to learn early on in high school to advocate for themselves before they attend college. In fact, students with disabilities at college who are most successful are knowledgeable about their disability and have good self-advocacy skills (Hamblin 2001). Hamblin also states that students transitioning to college need to understand that they are allowed accommodations under Section 504 and that the IEP is no longer valid, but getting those accommodations is entirely up to them. They have to learn to advocate for their own needs while in college.

The difference between a 504 and an IEP is significant, but that doesn't mean one is better than the other. Sometimes a 504 is the most appropriate for a student and sometimes it is the best alternative for a family who no longer wants to "fight" with the school.

CHAPTER 8

Communicating with the School

"Be mad at the problem, not the person."

I have been to all kinds of IEP meetings. There are the warm and fuzzy IEPs where everyone brings food, works together, respects each other, and does what it takes to provide the appropriate services. At the end we all hold hands and sing Kumbaya. Then there are very democratic, polite meetings that are measured but productive, where there might only be bottles of water on the table and friendly handshakes, but not a lot of socializing. Then there are the dictatorships. These are the tough, uncomfortable meetings where the school is making it clear that they are in charge, they are the experts, and, quite frankly, they have already determined the outcome of the meeting. This is when you need to be tough, not rude, but tough. I once attended an IEP meeting where the advocate yelled at the team, told them they didn't know what they were doing, and made two teachers cry. He used gotcha questioning techniques that are meant to catch people off guard, and intimidation. As an observer it was very uncomfortable and I don't think much was accomplished. It is very important to remember that teachers are not the problem; the problem is the fact that most of our educators do not receive the training they need to understand dyslexia. Teachers are doing the best they can with the information they have. Focus your energy on solving the problem, not demeaning the team. If you are looking for more gotcha tactics and yelling techniques, this is not the book for you.

Here are some tips on how to handle the IEP meeting where your voice is not being heard or you are not being permitted to contribute to the meeting in a meaningful way.

Ask questions, in fact, ask lots of questions

If you don't understand something or want to gather more information, just ask. Start questions with:

- Tell me more about…

    o Tell me more about how the program you are proposing will help a student with dyslexia?

- Can you please explain to me how…

    o Can you please explain to me how that goal will help my student close the achievement gap?

- How do you plan to…

    o How do you plan to teach orthographic awareness?

- Can you please explain to me who will…

    o Can you please explain to me who will be working with my child and what their training is with the program they will be using?

- Would it be possible to see the district's written policy about…

- Would it be possible to see the district's written policy about not qualifying a student for special education until they are two years behind?

One of the best techniques for information gathering is to ask the team to restate information. You can frame those questions the following ways:

- So, if I heard you correctly, you said…

- I'm not sure I understand, can you please elaborate on…

- I can't find that in the IDEA. Can you help find…

Don't be afraid of the D word

Say it, dyslexia. Say it again, dyslexia. Stand in the mirror and practice using the word, dyslexia. Now, when you get to that meeting, say dyslexia and say it often. On a weekly, if not daily, basis I hear someone complain that their district does not use the word dyslexia. Well, they might not use the word dyslexia, but what is stopping you from using it? Remember in Chapter 2 when it was pointed out that dyslexia is in the IDEA definition of specific learning difficulty (SLD)? You are free to use the word, so use it incessantly.

A little acknowledgement goes a long way

We all liked to be acknowledged when we are doing our best with the information we have, have good intentions, or are trying to be as compassionate as possible. So, when you get into an IEP meeting it might work in your student's favor to try to find places where you can acknowledge the team, or individual members of the team, for things they may be doing, or trying to do, to help your student.

For example, if a teacher has been particularly proactive in giving your student accommodations, even without an official IEP in place, you might want to thank him publicly for his efforts at the IEP team. If a resource teacher has gone out of his way to learn about dyslexia, you might want to acknowledge that you know he did that on their own time and, possibly, with their own money, and you appreciate it. Perhaps the only thing you can think of is to thank the IEP for the morning donuts, then do that. Remember that the people are not the problem (in most cases); the system is the problem.

You might also want to acknowledge to the team that you understand this must be very frustrating for them all. If you think about it, it must be very frustrating to be a teacher who genuinely cares about children and not have the tools needed to help them all. So, acknowledging that you understand this goes a long way. Don't get me wrong, this doesn't let the district off the hook for helping, but it does make the IEP meeting more productive and pleasant.

Self-assess behavior

As an advocate, I always approach IEP meetings as if I have to go back to that school in the morning and see the people on the team every day. I imagine that I have to send my student back to the teachers I just met with the next day. Then I ask myself, will my behavior negatively affect the relationship this family has with the school? Will my behavior affect how the student is treated? I want to leave that IEP meeting with the family and school relationship intact and positive, while also making sure that the student is receiving Free Appropriate Public Education (FAPE).

COMMUNICATION SCENARIOS

They read through the testing at a breakneck pace and seldom stop for your questions and clarifications.

It is important to remember that IEP teams hold these meetings all the time, so the language and scoring is second nature to them. But sometimes, I think they do it to prevent any questions or clarifications. For example, in one IEP meeting a CTOPP-2 score of 89 was presented and was labeled as average. When I politely pointed out that a score of 89 on the CTOPP-2 was actually below average the person scoffed and said, "I will change it, but it really isn't that important. Will it make you happy if I change it?" Well, yes, yes it would. Because it does matter, and if there are more careless mistakes like that, I will continue to point them out. There is a child on the other end of this IEP, so the details matter. This person also added that he was just using the general index of 80–115 being in the average range, and I should know that anyone conducting testing is required to use the labels set forth in the testing manual and they cannot change them, ever.

In this case, the way I communicated the error was important. It was important that it did not appear that I was accusing anyone of not doing their job correctly. My purpose was not to humiliate the person in front of the team. I did want to fix the issue, so instead I stated, "Help me understand why 89 is listed as average. If I remember correctly isn't 89 below average on the CTOPP-2?" Just a simple, quick note that was fixed and we all moved on, with a snarky comment from the team, but that is easily ignored.

As you sit down to the meeting, you are informed that you have one hour to complete the meeting and it needs to be completed by the end of that timeframe.

Never, ever feel rushed. This is a legal document that has great implications for your child. You might acknowledge that you understand the IEP team has a large, unmanageable caseload, but you would really appreciate it if they would agree to convene another meeting if you don't get done in the time allotted to make sure the IEP is as good as it can possibly be. So take your time. Ask questions. When the time is up, sign for attendance only, and schedule a second or even a third meeting until everything is right. Note that a few states do not require a parent signature to initiate the IEP, so make sure to check your state's regulations.

I know that these communication tips are easier said than done, especially when you are advocating for your own child, but give them a try and remember, it is okay to be emotional, this is your child and you can cry if you want or need to. There is no doubt that it can be really difficult to stand up for your rights in situations like these, but it is imperative that you stand your ground.

CHAPTER 9

Resources

Below is a list of carefully vetted resources that you can use to learn more about dyslexia and special education. Many parents have asked how to know which are good resources and which are resources to avoid. The general principle is that if any resource offers to "cure" dyslexia, you should avoid it. If any resource says it can help students with dyslexia in a set number of hours, you should avoid it. If a resource is offering advice based on their own personal experience and that is their only point of reference, you should avoid it.

United States special education regulations

Individuals with Disabilities Education Improvement Act— http://idea.ed.gov

Books
ADVOCACY

7 Steps for Success: High School to College Transition Strategies for Students with Disabilities, by Elizabeth C. Hamblin

All About IEPs, by Peter Wright, Pamela Darr Wright and Sandra Webb O'Connor

The Dyslexic Advantage: Unlocking the Hidden Potential of the Dyslexic Brain, by Drs. Brock and Fernette Eide

The Dyslexia Empowerment Plan: A Blueprint for Renewing Your Child's Confidence and Love of Learning, by Ben Foss

Essentials of Dyslexia Assessment and Intervention, by Nancy Mather and Barbara J. Wendling

Overcoming dyslexia: A New and Complete Science-Based Program for Reading Problems at any Level, by Sally Shaywitz

Proust and the Squid: The Story and Science of the Reading Brain, by Maryanne Wolf

Reading in the Brain: The New Science of How We Read, by Stanislaus Dehaene

Special Education Law, by Peter Wright and Pamela Darr Wright

When the School Says No, How to Get the Yes!: Securing Special Education Services for Your Child, by Vaughn Lauer

Wrightslaw: All About Tests and Assessments by Melissa Lee Farrall and Pamela Darr Wright

Wrightslaw: From Emotions to Advocacy: The Special Education Survival Guide, by Peter Wright and Pamela Darr Wright

DYSLEXIA

Bright Solutions for Dyslexia—www.dys-add.com

Decoding Dyslexia—www.decodingdyslexia.net

These websites list current advocacy efforts in your state.

Dyslexia Help—www.dyslexiahelp.umich.edu

Dyslexia Training Institute—www.dyslexiatraininginstitute.org

Embracing Dyslexia—www.embracingdyslexia.com

Headstrong Nation—www.headstrongnation.org

IEP Help—www.iephelp.com

International Dyslexia Association—www.interdys.org

Learning Ally—www.learningally.org

TED Ed, What is Dyslexia—www.youtube.com/watch?v=zafiGBr FkRM

Understood—www.understood.org

Wrightslaw—www.wrightslaw.com

The Yale Center for Dyslexia & Creativity—www.dyslexia.yale.edu

Simulation Kits

Dyslexia for a Day Simulation Kit, produced by Dyslexia Training Institute

How Difficult Can This Be? The FAT City Workshop with Rick Lavoie, produced by PBS

ADVOCACY

Dyslexia Training Institute, four-week course and certificate program available—www.dyslexiatraininginstitute.org

Wrightslaw Special Education Law and Advocacy—www.wrightslaw.com

IEP Help—www.iephelp.com

APPENDIX
IDEA REGULATIONS

Chapter 3 IDEA regulations in full
EDUCATIONAL RECORDS

If you want to inspect your student's records, whether it is before an IEP meeting or any other time, Section 300.613 provides you with the information you need to make those requests or support your requests.

Section 300.613 Access rights

(a) Each participating agency must permit parents to inspect and review any education records relating to their children that are collected, maintained, or used by the agency under this part. The agency must comply with a request without unnecessary delay and before any meeting regarding an IEP, or any hearing pursuant to Section 300.507 or Sections 300.530 through 300.532, or resolution session pursuant to Section 300.510, and in no case more than 45 days after the request has been made.

(b) The right to inspect and review education records under this section includes

   (1) The right to a response from the participating agency to reasonable requests for explanations and interpretations of the records;

   (2) The right to request that the agency provide copies of the records containing the information if failure to provide those copies

would effectively prevent the parent from exercising the right to inspect and review the records; and

(3) The right to have a representative of the parent inspect and review the records.

(c) An agency may presume that the parent has authority to inspect and review records relating to his or her child unless the agency has been advised that the parent does not have the authority under applicable State law governing such matters as guardianship, separation, and divorce.

THE D WORD

Section 300.8 is the definition of how the IDEA defines a child with a disability. This is also where you will find the word *dyslexia* included in this definition. Dyslexia has been in this definition since the inception of the IDEA. In some states there is a separate definition of dyslexia.

Section 300.8 Child with a disability

(c) (10) Child with a disability. Specific learning disability.

(i) General. Specific learning disability means a disorder in one or more of the basic psychological processes involved in understanding or in using language, spoken or written, that may manifest itself in the imperfect ability to listen, think, speak, read, write, spell, or to do mathematical calculations, including conditions such as perceptual disabilities, brain injury, minimal brain dysfunction, dyslexia, and developmental aphasia.

EVALUATIONS

When requesting an evaluation Section 614 (a) (1) (B) describes who may initiate the assessment process and who will conduct the assessment. Remember all requests need to be in writing.

Section 614(a)(1)(B) Evaluations, eligibility determinations, Individualized Education Programs, and educational placements

(a) Evaluations, Parental Consent, and Reevaluations.

(1) Initial evaluations.

(A) In general. A State educational agency, other State agency, or local educational agency shall conduct a full and individual initial evaluation in accordance with this paragraph and subsection (b), before the initial provision of special education and related services to a child with a disability under this part.

(B) Request for initial evaluation. Consistent with subparagraph (D), either a parent of a child, or a State educational agency, other State agency, or local educational agency may initiate a request for an initial evaluation to determine if the child is a child with a disability.

PRIOR WRITTEN NOTICE (PWN)

If you have made a request or the school is proposing a change in services, the school must provide you with a notice that should include an explanation, as outlined in Section 300.503.

Section 300.503 Prior notice by the public agency; content of notice

(a) Notice. Written notice that meets the requirements of paragraph (b) of this section must be given to the parents of a child with a disability a reasonable time before the public agency

(1) Proposes to initiate or change the identification, evaluation, or educational placement of the child or the provision of FAPE to the child; or

(2) Refuses to initiate or change the identification, evaluation, or educational placement of the child or the provision of FAPE to the child.

(b) Content of notice. The notice required under paragraph (a) of this section must include

(1) A description of the action proposed or refused by the agency;

(2) An explanation of why the agency proposes or refuses to take the action;

(3) A description of each evaluation procedure, assessment, record, or report the agency used as a basis for the proposed or refused action;

(4) A statement that the parents of a child with a disability have protection under the procedural safeguards of this part and, if this notice is not an initial referral for evaluation, the means by which a copy of a description of the procedural safeguards can be obtained;

(5) Sources for parents to contact to obtain assistance in understanding the provisions of this part;

(6) A description of other options that the IEP Team considered and the reasons why those options were rejected;

(7) A description of other factors that are relevant to the agency's proposal or refusal.

(c) Notice in understandable language.

(1) The notice required under paragraph (a) of this section must be (i) Written in language understandable to the general public; and (ii) Provided in the native language of the parent or other mode of communication used by the parent, unless it is clearly not feasible to do so.

(2) If the native language or other mode of communication of the parent is not a written language, the public agency must take steps to ensure (i) That the notice is translated orally or by other means to the parent in his or her native language or other mode of communication; (ii) That the parent understands the content of the notice; and (iii) That there is written evidence that the requirements in paragraphs (c)(2)(i) and (ii) of this section have been met.

EVALUATION PROCEDURES

Once a request for an assessment has been approved Section 300.304(a) outlines what the evaluation shall include.

Section 300.304(a) Evaluation procedures

(a) Notice. The public agency must provide notice to the parents of a child with a disability, in accordance with Section 300.503, that describes any evaluation procedures the agency proposes to conduct.

(b) Conduct of evaluation. In conducting the evaluation, the public agency must

(1) Use a variety of assessment tools and strategies to gather relevant functional, developmental, and academic information about the child, including information provided by the parent, that may assist in determining (i) Whether the child is a child with a disability under Section 300.8; and (ii) The content of the child's IEP, including information related to enabling the child to be involved in and progress in the general education curriculum (or for a preschool child, to participate in appropriate activities);

(2) Not use any single measure or assessment as the sole criterion for determining whether a child is a child with a disability and for determining an appropriate educational program for the child;

(3) Use technically sound instruments that may assess the relative contribution of cognitive and behavioral factors, in addition to physical or developmental factors.

(c) Other evaluation procedures. Each public agency must ensure that

(1) Assessments and other evaluation materials used to assess a child under this part (i) are selected and administered so as not to be discriminatory on a racial or cultural basis; (ii) are provided and administered in the child's native language or other mode of communication and in the form most likely to yield accurate information on what the child knows and can do academically, developmentally, and functionally, unless it is clearly not feasible to so provide or administer; (iii) Are used for the purposes for which the assessments or measures are valid and reliable; (iv) Are administered by trained and knowledgeable personnel; and (v) Are administered in accordance with any instructions provided by the producer of the assessments.

(2) Assessments and other evaluation materials include those tailored to assess specific areas of educational need and not merely those that are designed to provide a single general intelligence quotient.

(3) Assessments are selected and administered so as best to ensure that if an assessment is administered to a child with impaired sensory, manual, or speaking skills, the assessment results accurately reflect the child's aptitude or achievement level or whatever other factors the test purports to measure, rather than reflecting the child's impaired sensory, manual, or speaking skills (unless those skills are the factors that the test purports to measure).

(4) The child is assessed in all areas related to the suspected disability, including, if appropriate, health, vision, hearing, social and emotional status, general intelligence, academic performance, communicative status, and motor abilities.

(5) Assessments of children with disabilities who transfer from one public agency to another public agency in the same school year are coordinated with those children's prior and subsequent schools, as necessary and as expeditiously as possible, consistent with Section 300.301(d)(2) and (e), to ensure prompt completion of full evaluations.

(6) In evaluating each child with a disability under Sections 300.304 through 300.306, the evaluation is sufficiently comprehensive to

identify all of the child's special education and related services needs, whether or not commonly linked to the disability category in which the child has been classified.

(7) Assessment tools and strategies that provide relevant information that directly assists persons in determining the educational needs of the child are provided.

ASSISTIVE TECHNOLOGY

Section 300.6 describes what assistive technology (AT) means in the special education situation. This also includes the stipulation that an AT evaluation is necessary to determine how the AT will respond to the child's needs.

Section 300.6 Assistive technology service. This means any service that directly assists a child with a disability in the selection, acquisition, or use of an AT device. The term includes (a) The evaluation of the needs of a child with a disability, including a functional evaluation of the child in the child's customary environment.

INITIAL EVALUATION

The initial evaluation must be completed within a designated timeline (check your state for timelines). Section 300.301 provides the timeline and also describes when exceptions to timelines are acceptable.

Section 300.301 Initial evaluations

(a) General. Each public agency must conduct a full and individual initial evaluation, in accordance with Section 300.305 and 300.306, before the initial provision of special education and related services to a child with a disability under this part.

b) Request for initial evaluation. Consistent with the consent requirements in Section 300.300, either a parent of a child or a public agency may initiate a request for an initial evaluation to determine if the child is a child with a disability.

(c) Procedures for initial evaluation. The initial evaluation

(1) (i) Must be conducted within 60 days of receiving parental consent for the evaluation; or (ii) If the State establishes a timeframe within which the evaluation must be conducted, within that timeframe;

(2) Must consist of procedures (i) To determine if the child is a child with a disability under Section 300.8; and (ii) To determine the educational needs of the child.

(d) Exception. The timeframe described in paragraph (c)(1) of this section does not apply to a public agency if

(1) The parent of a child repeatedly fails or refuses to produce the child for the evaluation; or

(2) A child enrolls in a school of another public agency after the relevant timeframe in paragraph (c)(1) of this section has begun, and prior to a determination by the child's previous public agency as to whether the child is a child with a disability under Section 300.8.

(e) The exception in paragraph (d)(2) of this section applies only if the subsequent public agency is making sufficient progress to ensure a prompt completion of the evaluation, and the parent and subsequent public agency agree to a specific time when the evaluation will be completed.

Chapter 4 IDEA regulations in full
EDUCATIONAL RECORDS

If you want to inspect your student's records, whether it is before an IEP meeting or any other time, Section 300.613 provides you with the information you need to make those requests or support your requests.

Section 300.613 Access rights

(a) Each participating agency must permit parents to inspect and review any education records relating to their children that are collected, maintained, or used by the agency under this part. The agency must comply with a request without unnecessary delay and before any meeting regarding an IEP, or any hearing pursuant to Section 300.507 or Sections 300.530 through 300.532, or resolution session pursuant to Section 300.510, and in no case more than 45 days after the request has been made.

(b) The right to inspect and review education records under this section includes

(1) The right to a response from the participating agency to reasonable requests for explanations and interpretations of the records;

(2) The right to request that the agency provide copies of the records containing the information if failure to provide those copies would effectively prevent the parent from exercising the right to inspect and review the records;

(3) The right to have a representative of the parent inspect and review the records.

(c) An agency may presume that the parent has authority to inspect and review records relating to his or her child unless the agency has been advised that the parent does not have the authority under applicable State law governing such matters as guardianship, separation, and divorce.

IEP TEAM

The members of the IEP Team are very important to building a successful IEP for your student. Section 300.321 describes who needs to be at the IEP meeting and when it is permissible for an IEP Team member not to be present. Section 300.321 also describes how a parent or guardian can excuse a team member.

Section 300.321 IEP Team

General. The public agency must ensure that the IEP Team for each child with a disability includes

(1) The parents of the child;

(2) Not less than one regular education teacher of the child (if the child is, or may be, participating in the regular education environment);

(3) Not less than one special education teacher of the child, or where appropriate, not less then one special education provider of the child;

(4) A representative of the public agency who (i) Is qualified to provide, or supervise the provision of, specially designed instruction to meet the unique needs of children with disabilities; (ii) Is knowledgeable about the general education curriculum; and (iii) Is knowledgeable about the availability of resources of the public agency.

(5) An individual who can interpret the instructional implications of evaluation results, who may be a member of the team described in paragraphs (a)(2) through (a)(6) of this section;

(6) At the discretion of the parent or the agency, other individuals who have knowledge or special expertise regarding the child, including related services personnel as appropriate; and

(7) Whenever appropriate, the child with a disability.

(b) Transition services participants.

    (1) In accordance with paragraph (a)(7) of this section, the public agency must invite a child with a disability to attend the child's IEP Team meeting if a purpose of the meeting will be the consideration of the postsecondary goals for the child and the transition services needed to assist the child in reaching those goals under Section 300.320(b).

    (2) If the child does not attend the IEP Team meeting, the public agency must take other steps to ensure that the child's preferences and interests are considered.

    (3) To the extent appropriate, with the consent of the parents or a child who has reached the age of majority, in implementing the requirements of paragraph (b)(1) of this section, the public agency must invite a representative of any participating agency that is likely to be responsible for providing or paying for transition services.

(c) Determination of knowledge and special expertise. The determination of the knowledge or special expertise of any individual described in paragraph (a)(6) of this section must be made by the party (parents or public agency) who invited the individual to be a member of the IEP Team.

(d) Designating a public agency representative. A public agency may designate a public agency member of the IEP Team to also serve as the agency representative, if the criteria in paragraph (a)(4) of this section are satisfied.

(e) IEP Team attendance.

    (1) A member of the IEP Team described in paragraphs (a)(2) through (a)(5) of this section is not required to attend an IEP Team meeting, in whole or in part, if the parent of a child with a disability and the public agency agree, in writing, that the attendance of the member is not necessary because the member's area of the curriculum or related services is not being modified or discussed in the meeting.

    (2) A member of the IEP Team described in paragraph (e)(1) of this section may be excused from attending an IEP Team meeting, in whole or in part, when the meeting involves a modification to or discussion of the member's area of the curriculum or related services, if (i) The parent, in writing, and the public agency consent to the excusal; and (ii) The member submits, in writing

to the parent and the IEP Team, input into the development of the IEP prior to the meeting.

(f) Initial IEP Team meeting for child under Part C. In the case of a child who was previously served under Part C of the Act, an invitation to the initial IEP Team meeting must, at the request of the parent, be sent to the Part C service coordinator or other representatives of the Part C system to assist with the smooth transition of services.

EVALUATION PROCEDURES

Once a request for an assessment has been approved Section 300.304(a) outlines what the evaluation shall include.

Section 300.304(b)(1) Evaluation procedures

(b) (1) Use a variety of assessment tools and strategies to gather relevant functional, developmental, and academic information about the child, including information provided by the parent, which may assist in determining (i) Whether the child is a child with a disability under Section 300.8; and (ii) The content of the child's IEP, including information related to enabling the child to be involved in and progress in the general education curriculum (or for a preschool child, to participate in appropriate activities);

(2) Not use any single measure or assessment as the sole criterion for determining whether a child is a child with a disability and for determining an appropriate educational program for the child;

(3) Use technically sound instruments that may assess the relative contribution of cognitive and behavioral factors, in addition to physical or developmental factors.

(c) Other evaluation procedures. Each public agency must ensure that

(1) Assessments and other evaluation materials used to assess a child under this part (i) Are selected and administered so as not to be discriminatory on a racial or cultural basis; (ii) Are provided and administered in the child's native language or other mode of communication and in the form most likely to yield accurate information on what the child knows and can do academically, developmentally, and functionally, unless it is clearly not feasible to so provide or administer; (iii) Are used for the purposes for which the assessments or measures are valid and reliable; (iv) Are administered by trained and knowledgeable personnel;

and (v) Are administered in accordance with any instructions provided by the producer of the assessments.

(2) Assessments and other evaluation materials include those tailored to assess specific areas of educational need and not merely those that are designed to provide a single general intelligence quotient.

(3) Assessments are selected and administered so as best to ensure that if an assessment is administered to a child with impaired sensory, manual, or speaking skills, the assessment results accurately reflect the child's aptitude or achievement level or whatever other factors the test purports to measure, rather than reflecting the child's impaired sensory, manual, or speaking skills (unless those skills are the factors that the test purports to measure).

(4) The child is assessed in all areas related to the suspected disability, including, if appropriate, health, vision, hearing, social and emotional status, general intelligence, academic performance, communicative status, and motor abilities.

(5) Assessments of children with disabilities who transfer from one public agency to another public agency in the same school year are coordinated with those children's prior and subsequent schools, as necessary and as expeditiously as possible, consistent with Section 300.301(d)(2) and (e), to ensure prompt completion of full evaluations.

(6) In evaluating each child with a disability under Sections 300.304 through 300.306, the evaluation is sufficiently comprehensive to identify all of the child's special education and related services needs, whether or not commonly linked to the disability category in which the child has been classified.

(7) Assessment tools and strategies that provide relevant information that directly assists persons in determining the educational needs of the child are provided.

DETERMINATION OF A SPECIFIC LEARNING DISABILITY (SLD)

To be eligible for special education services, the IEP team must first determine if the student has a disability. In the case of SLD, the team can make this determination using a combination of information. Most importantly, Section 300.307(a) outlines that a "severe discrepancy" is not required to determine if the child qualifies under SLD.

Section 300.307(a) Specific Learning Disabilities

(a) A State must adopt, consistent with Section 300.309, criteria for determining whether a child has a specific learning disability as defined in Section 300.8(c)(10). In addition, the criteria adopted by the State

(1) Must not require the use of a severe discrepancy between intellectual ability and achievement for determining whether a child has a specific learning disability, as defined in Section 300.8(c)(10);

(2) Must permit the use of a process based on the child's response to scientific, research-based intervention;

(3) May permit the use of other alternative research-based procedures for determining whether a child has a specific learning disability, as defined in Section 300.8(c)(10).

(b) Consistency with State criteria. A public agency must use the State criteria adopted pursuant to paragraph (a) of this section in determining whether a child has a specific learning disability.

OBSERVING THE STUDENT DURING AN EVALUATION

During an assessment to determine eligibility for special education services the assessor must conduct an evaluation of the student in "the child's learning environment." In the case of dyslexia, this should include an observation of the work produced. Section 300.310 describes what should be included in an observation.

Section 300.310 Observation

(a) The public agency must ensure that the child is observed in the child's learning environment (including the regular classroom setting) to document the child's academic performance and behavior in the areas of difficulty.

(b) The group described in Section 300.306(a)(1), in determining whether a child has a specific learning disability, must decide to

(1) Use information from an observation in routine classroom instruction and monitoring of the child's performance that was done before the child was referred for an evaluation; or

(2) Have at least one member of the group described in Section 300.306(a)(1) conduct an observation of the child's academic performance in the regular classroom after the child has been

referred for an evaluation and parental consent, consistent with Section 300.300(a), is obtained.

(c) In the case of a child of less than school age or out of school, a group member must observe the child in an environment appropriate for a child of that age.

INDEPENDENT EVALUATIONS

When you disagree with the evaluation conducted by the school, you can request an Independent Educational Evaluation (IEE) at the expense of the district. Section 300.502 describes how to request and obtain an IEE. If the district denies the IEE request Section 300.502 outlines that the school must file due process.

Section 300.502 Independent Educational Evaluation

(a) General.

(1) The parents of a child with a disability have the right under this part to obtain an Independent Educational Evaluation (IEE) of the child, subject to paragraphs (b) through (e) of this section.

(2) Each public agency must provide to parents, upon request for an IEE, information about where an IEE may be obtained, and the agency criteria applicable for IEEs as set forth in paragraph (e) of this section.

(3) For the purposes of this subpart (i) IEE means an evaluation conducted by a qualified examiner who is not employed by the public agency responsible for the education of the child in question; and (ii) Public expense means that the public agency either pays for the full cost of the evaluation or ensures that the evaluation is otherwise provided at no cost to the parent, consistent with Section 300.103.

(b) Parent right to evaluation at public expense.

(1) A parent has the right to an IEE at public expense if the parent disagrees with an evaluation obtained by the public agency, subject to the conditions in paragraphs (b)(2) through (4) of this section.

(2) If a parent requests an IEE at public expense, the public agency must, without unnecessary delay, either (i) File a due process complaint to request a hearing to show that its evaluation is appropriate; or (ii) Ensure that an IEE is provided at public expense, unless the agency demonstrates in a hearing pursuant

to Sections 300.507 through 300.513 that the evaluation obtained by the parent did not meet agency criteria.

(3) If the public agency files a due process complaint notice to request a hearing and the final decision is that the agency's evaluation is appropriate, the parent still has the right to an IEE, but not at public expense.

(4) If a parent requests an IEE, the public agency may ask for the parent's reason why he or she objects to the public evaluation. However, the public agency may not require the parent to provide an explanation and may not unreasonably delay either providing the IEE at public expense or filing a due process complaint to request a due process hearing to defend the public evaluation.

(5) A parent is entitled to only one IEE at public expense each time the public agency conducts an evaluation with which the parent disagrees.

(c) Parent-initiated evaluations. If the parent obtains an IEE at public expense or shares with the public agency an evaluation obtained at private expense, the results of the evaluation

(1) Must be considered by the public agency, if it meets agency criteria, in any decision made with respect to the provision of FAPE to the child; and

(2) May be presented by any party as evidence at a hearing on a due process complaint under subpart E of this part regarding that child.

(d) Requests for evaluations by hearing officers. If a hearing officer requests an IEE as part of a hearing on a due process complaint, the cost of the evaluation must be at public expense.

(e) Agency criteria.

(1) If an IEE is at public expense, the criteria under which the evaluation is obtained, including the location of the evaluation and the qualifications of the examiner, must be the same as the criteria that the public agency uses when it initiates an evaluation, to the extent those criteria are consistent with the parent's right to an IEE.

(2) Except for the criteria described in paragraph (e)(1) of this section, a public agency may not impose conditions or timelines related to obtaining an IEE at public expense.

HOW TO DETERMINE ELIGIBILITY

Once the evaluation has been conducted the IEP team meets to determine eligibility. This should not be done prior to the meeting or without parent involvement in the decision. Section 300.306 describes how this process should take place during a meeting. It also includes eligibility criteria, which includes the clarification that a severe discrepancy is not the only determining factor and must "Draw upon information from a variety of sources, including aptitude and achievement tests, parent input, and teacher recommendations, as well as information about the child's physical condition, social or cultural background, and adaptive behavior; and (ii) Ensure that information obtained from all of these sources is documented and carefully considered."

Section 300.306 Determination of eligibility

(a) General. Upon completion of the administration of assessments and other evaluation measures

    (1) A group of qualified professionals and the parent of the child determines whether the child is a child with a disability, as defined in Section 300.8, in accordance with paragraph (b) of this section and the educational needs of the child; and

    (2) The public agency provides a copy of the evaluation report and the documentation of determination of eligibility at no cost to the parent.

(b) Special rule for eligibility determination. A child must not be determined to be a child with a disability under this part

    (1) If the determinant factor for that determination is (i) Lack of appropriate instruction in reading, including the essential components of reading instruction (as defined in Section 1208(3) of the Elementary and Secondary Education Act); (ii) Lack of appropriate instruction in math; or (iii) Limited English proficiency; and (2) If the child does not otherwise meet the eligibility criteria under Section 300.8(a).

(c) Procedures for determining eligibility and educational need.

    (1) In interpreting evaluation data for the purpose of determining if a child is a child with a disability under Section 300.8, and the educational needs of the child, each public agency must (i) Draw upon information from a variety of sources, including aptitude and achievement tests, parent input, and teacher recommendations, as well as information about the child's

physical condition, social or cultural background, and adaptive behavior; and (ii) Ensure that information obtained from all of these sources is documented and carefully considered.

(2) If a determination is made that a child has a disability and needs special education and related services, an IEP must be developed for the child in accordance with Sections 300.320 through 300.324.

IS IT A SPECIFIC LEARNING DISABILITY?

When a student is assessed for SLD, the areas that need to be assessed are listed in Section 300.309. This also describes any situations, such as "(i) A visual, hearing, or motor disability; (ii) Mental retardation; (iii) Emotional disturbance; (iv) Cultural factors; (v) Environmental or economic disadvantage; or (vi) Limited English proficiency." This might be the reason for the academic difficultly and not SLD.

Section 300.309 Determining the existence of a specific learning disability

(a) The group described in Section 300.306 may determine that a child has a specific learning disability, as defined in Section 300.8(c)(10), if

(1) The child does not achieve adequately for the child's age or to meet State-approved grade-level standards in one or more of the following areas, when provided with learning experiences and instruction appropriate for the child's age or State-approved grade-level standards: (i) Oral expression. (ii) Listening comprehension. (iii) Written expression. (iv) Basic reading skill. (v) Reading fluency skills. (vi) Reading comprehension. (vii) Mathematics calculation. (viii) Mathematics problem solving.

(2) (i) The child does not make sufficient progress to meet age or State-approved grade-level standards in one or more of the areas identified in paragraph (a)(1) of this section when using a process based on the child's response to scientific, research-based intervention; or (ii) The child exhibits a pattern of strengths and weaknesses in performance, achievement, or both, relative to age, State-approved grade-level standards, or intellectual development, that is determined by the group to be relevant to the identification of a specific learning disability, using appropriate assessments, consistent with Sections 300.304 and 300.305; and

3) The group determines that its findings under paragraphs (a)(1) and (2) of this section are not primarily the result of (i) A visual,

hearing, or motor disability; (ii) Mental retardation; (iii) Emotional disturbance; (iv) Cultural factors; (v) Environmental or economic disadvantage; or (vi) Limited English proficiency.

(b) To ensure that underachievement in a child suspected of having a specific learning disability is not due to lack of appropriate instruction in reading or math, the group must consider, as part of the evaluation described in Sections 300.304 through 300.306

  (1) Data that demonstrate that prior to, or as a part of, the referral process, the child was provided appropriate instruction in regular education settings, delivered by qualified personnel; and

  (2) Data-based documentation of repeated assessments of achievement at reasonable intervals, reflecting formal assessment of student progress during instruction, which was provided to the child's parents.

(c) The public agency must promptly request parental consent to evaluate the child to determine if the child needs special education and related services, and must adhere to the timeframes described in Sections 300.301 and 300.303, unless extended by mutual written agreement of the child's parents and a group of qualified professionals, as described in Section 300.306(a)(1)

  (1) If, prior to a referral, a child has not made adequate progress after an appropriate period of time when provided instruction, as described in paragraphs (b)(1) and (b)(2) of this section; and

  (2) Whenever a child is referred for an evaluation.

Chapter 5 IDEA regulations in full
WHAT IS AN IEP?

Once a student has been determined to qualify for special education services, the team needs to create an Individualized Education Program (IEP). Section 300.320 outlines what needs to be included in an IEP document.

Section 300.320 Definition of Individualized Education Program

(a) General. As used in this part, the term individualized education program or IEP means a written statement for each child with a disability that is developed, reviewed, and revised in a meeting in accordance with Sections 300.320 through 300.324, and that must include

(1) A statement of the child's present levels of academic achievement and functional performance, including (i) How the child's disability affects the child's involvement and progress in the general education curriculum (i.e., the same curriculum as for nondisabled children); or (ii) For preschool children, as appropriate, how the disability affects the child's participation in appropriate activities;

(2) (i) A statement of measurable annual goals, including academic and functional goals designed to (A) Meet the child's needs that result from the child's disability to enable the child to be involved in and make progress in the general education curriculum; and (B) Meet each of the child's other educational needs that result from the child's disability;

(ii) For children with disabilities who take alternate assessments aligned to alternate achievement standards, a description of benchmarks or short-term objectives;

(3) A description of (i) How the child's progress toward meeting the annual goals described in paragraph (2) of this section will be measured; and (ii) When periodic reports on the progress the child is making toward meeting the annual goals (such as through the use of quarterly or other periodic reports, concurrent with the issuance of report cards) will be provided;

(4) A statement of the special education and related services and supplementary aids and services, based on peer-reviewed research to the extent practicable, to be provided to the child, or on behalf of the child, and a statement of the program modifications or supports for school personnel that will be provided to enable the child (i) To advance appropriately toward attaining the annual goals; (ii) To be involved in and make progress in the general education curriculum in accordance with paragraph (a)(1) of this section, and to participate in extracurricular and other nonacademic activities; and (iii) To be educated and participate with other children with disabilities and nondisabled children in the activities described in this section;

(5) An explanation of the extent, if any, to which the child will not participate with nondisabled children in the regular class and in the activities described in paragraph (a)(4) of this section;

(6) (i) A statement of any individual appropriate accommodations that are necessary to measure the academic achievement and

functional performance of the child on State and district-wide assessments consistent with section 612(a)(16) of the Act; and (ii) If the IEP Team determines that the child must take an alternate assessment instead of a particular regular State or district-wide assessment of student achievement, a statement of why (A) The child cannot participate in the regular assessment; and (B) The particular alternate assessment selected is appropriate for the child; and

(7) The projected date for the beginning of the services and modifications described in paragraph (a)(4) of this section, and the anticipated frequency, location, and duration of those services and modifications.

(b) Transition services. Beginning not later than the first IEP to be in effect when the child turns 16, or younger if determined appropriate by the IEP Team, and updated annually, thereafter, the IEP must include

(1) Appropriate measurable postsecondary goals based upon age appropriate transition assessments related to training, education, employment, and, where appropriate, independent living skills; and

(2) The transition services (including courses of study) needed to assist the child in reaching those goals.

(c) Transfer of rights at age of majority. Beginning not later than one year before the child reaches the age of majority under State law, the IEP must include a statement that the child has been informed of the child's rights under Part B of the Act, if any, that will transfer to the child on reaching the age of majority under Section 300.520.

(d) Construction. Nothing in this section shall be construed to require

(1) That additional information be included in a child's IEP beyond what is explicitly required in Section 614 of the Act; or

(2) The IEP Team to include information under one component of a child's IEP that is already contained under another component of the child's IEP.

IF YOUR STUDENT NEEDS RELATED SERVICES

Often a student with SLD will have co-existing conditions, such as dysgraphia and/or speech difficulties, and students are provided with services for these conditions. Section 300.34 describes which services fall into the related services category.

Section 300.34 Related services

(a) General. Related services means transportation and such developmental, corrective, and other supportive services as are required to assist a child with a disability to benefit from special education, and includes speech and language pathology and audiology services, interpreting services, psychological services, physical and occupational therapy, recreation, including therapeutic recreation, early identification and assessment of disabilities in children, counseling services, including rehabilitation counseling, orientation and mobility services, and medical services for diagnostic or evaluation purposes. Related services also include school health services and school nurse services, social work services in schools, and parent counseling and training.

Chapter 6 IDEA regulations in full
EVALUATIONS

When you are requesting an evaluation, Section 614 (a) (1) (B) describes who may initiate the assessment process and who will conduct the assessment. Remember, all requests need to be in writing.

Section 614 (d) (4) (a) (i) Evaluations, eligibility determinations, Individualized Education Programs, and educational placements

(4) Review and revision of IEP (A) In general. The local educational agency shall ensure that, subject to subparagraph (B), the IEP Team (i) reviews the child's IEP periodically, but not less frequently than annually, to determine whether the annual goals for the child are being achieved; and (ii) revises the IEP as appropriate to address (I) any lack of expected progress toward the annual goals and in the general education curriculum, where appropriate; (II) the results of any reevaluation conducted under this section; (III) information about the child provided to, or by, the parents, as described in subsection (c)(1)(B); (IV) the child's anticipated needs; or (V) other matters. (B) Requirement with respect to regular education teacher. A regular education teacher of the child, as a member of the IEP Team, shall, consistent with paragraph (1)(C), participate in the review and revision of the IEP of the child.

REFERENCES

Dehaene, Stanislaus (2010) *Reading in the Brain: The New Science of How We Read.* New York: Penguin Books.

Dehaene, Stanislaus (2011) "Reading as Neuronal Recycling: A Universal Brain Organization Underlying Reading Acquisition." In P. McCardle, B. Miller, J.R. Lee, Jun Ren, & O.J.L.Tzeng (eds) *Dyslexia Across Languages Orthography and the Brain-Gene-Behavior Link* (pp.102–116). Baltimore, MD: Paul H. Brookes Publishing Co.

Foss, Ben (2013) *The Dyslexia Empowerment Plan: A Blueprint for Renewing Your Child's Confidence and Love of Learning.* New York: Ballantine Books.

Hamblin, Elizabeth (2011) *7 Steps for Success: High School to College Transition Strategies for Students with Disabilities.* Arlington, VA: Council for Exceptional Children.

Lyon, G.R., Fletcher, J.M., Shaywitz, B., and Shaywitz, S.E., *et al.* (2001) "Rethinking Learning Disabilities." In C.R. Hokanson (ed.) *Rethinking Special Education for a New Century.* Washington, DC: Thomas B. Fordham Foundation and Progressive Policy Institute.

Shaywitz, Sally (2003) *Overcoming Dyslexia: A New and Complete Science-Based Program for Reading Problems at Any Level.* New York: Alfred A. Knopf.

Wolf, Maryanne (2008) *Proust and the Squid: The Story and Science of the Reading Brain.* Cambridge: Icon Books Ltd.

Websites

American Academy of Opthalmologists—http://one.aao.org/clinical-statement/joint-statement-learning-disabilities-dyslexia-vis

International Dyslexia Association Matrix — http://eida.org/?s=matrix

Lexicon Valley, The Schwa is the Laziest Sound in All of Human Speech—

www.slate.com/blogs/lexicon_valley/2014/06/05/schwa_the_word_for_the_most_comcom_vowel_sound_in_english_comes_from_hebrew.html

Office of Special Education and Rehabilitative Services memo, January 21, 2011—www2.ed.gov/policy/speced/guid/idea/memosdcltrs/osep11-07rtimemo.pdf

Office of Special Education and Rehabilitative Services memo, October 23, 2015—www2.ed.gov/policy/speced/guid/idea/memosdcltrs/guidance-on-dyslexia-10-2015.pdf

Office Special Education Programs (OSEP), Letter to Delisle, December 13, 2013—www2.ed.gov/policy/speced/guid/idea/memosdcltrs/13-008520r-sc-delisle-twiceexceptional.pdf

Office of Special Education, clarification letter for audio recordings in IEP meetings—Officewww2.ed.gov/policy/speced/guid/idea/letters/2003-2/redact060403iep2q2003.pdf

Rachel's English, English: A Stressed-Time Language—http://rachelsenglish.com/english-stress-timed-language/

United States Department of Education Office of Special Education Programs—www2.ed.gov/policy/speced/guid/idea/memosdcltrs/osep11-07rtimemo.pdf

INDEX